CHIP-CARVING GOURDS

ADVANCED TECHNIQUES

Marilyn Rehm

4880 Lower Valley Road · Atglen, PA · 19310

Other Schiffer Books by Marilyn Rehm
A Guide to Chip-Carving Gourds, 978-0-7643-3210-4, $14.99

Other Schiffer Books on Related Subjects
Gourd Art Basics: The Complete Guide to Cleaning, Preparation, & Repair, 978-0-7643-2829-9, $14.95
Coiled Designs for Gourd Art, 978-0-7643-3011-7, $14.99
Decorating Gourds: Carving, Burning, Painting, & More, 0-7643-1312-6, $14.95

Copyright © 2009 by Marilyn Rehm
Library of Congress Control Number: 2009926628

All rights reserved. No part of this work may be reproduced or used in any form or by any means—graphic, electronic, or mechanical, including photocopying or information storage and retrieval systems—without written permission from the publisher.
The scanning, uploading and distribution of this book or any part thereof via the Internet or via any other means without the permission of the publisher is illegal and punishable by law. Please purchase only authorized editions and do not participate in or encourage the electronic piracy of copyrighted materials.
"Schiffer," "Schiffer Publishing Ltd. & Design," and the "Design of pen and ink well" are registered trademarks of Schiffer Publishing Ltd.

Designed by RoS
Type set in Bremen Bd BT/NewBskvll BT

ISBN: 978-0-7643-3289-0
Printed in China

Schiffer Books are available at special discounts for bulk purchases for sales promotions or premiums. Special editions, including personalized covers, corporate imprints, and excerpts can be created in large quantities for special needs. For more information contact the publisher:

Published by Schiffer Publishing Ltd.
4880 Lower Valley Road
Atglen, PA 19310
Phone: (610) 593-1777; Fax: (610) 593-2002
E-mail: Info@schifferbooks.com

For the largest selection of fine reference books on this and related subjects, please visit our web site at:
www.schifferbooks.com
We are always looking for people to write books on new and related subjects. If you have an idea for a book please contact us at the above address.

This book may be purchased from the publisher.
Include $5.00 for shipping.
Please try your bookstore first.
You may write for a free catalog.

In Europe, Schiffer books are distributed by
Bushwood Books
6 Marksbury Ave.
Kew Gardens
Surrey TW9 4JF England
Phone: 44 (0) 20 8392 8585;
Fax: 44 (0) 20 8392 9876
E-mail: info@bushwood-books.co.uk
Website: www.bushwood-books.co.uk

ACKNOWLEDGMENTS

I am very fortunate to be in the middle of three generations of family who have worked with gourds and I have been continually encouraged to grow, show, and teach. The American Gourd Society publishes a full color magazine, and state chapters sponsor gourd shows with workshops to introduce gourds to the public. With the recent increased interest in gourds, growers and seedsmen have worked to provide more variety and quality of gourds available to crafters.

A special thanks to David Stichweh for his patience as well as technical skill in photographing the carving projects in this book.

CONTENTS

INTRODUCTION 6

CHAPTER ONE: GETTING STARTED 7
    Choosing Gouges 7
    Selecting Gourds 8
    Additional Tools and Supplies 8

CHAPTER TWO: CARVING LINES 10
    Triangle Bowl Pattern 10
    Star Pattern Birdhouse 14
    Basket Project 17
    Southwestern Pattern 20

CHAPTER THREE: COMBINING LINES AND CHIPS 25
    Circular Pattern Birdhouse 26

CHAPTER FOUR: TWO-TONE CARVING 31
    Triangle Outline Bowl 31
    Horizontal Bands 33
    Diagonal Bands 35
    A New Fill Pattern 37

CHAPTER FIVE: BEYOND BOWLS AND BIRDHOUSES 40
    Vases 40
    Oil Lamps 41
    Magnifiers, Kaleidoscopes, & Mini-lights 42
    Jewelry! 43
    Two-dimensional Ornaments 43

CHAPTER SIX: TROUBLESHOOTING AND DESIGN 44
    Mold Mosaic 44
    Big Gourds 46
    Long Gourds 47
    Tiny Gourds 48
    A Pre-cut Basket 49

CHAPTER SEVEN: TIPS AND TRICKS 51

CHAPTER EIGHT: GALLERY 56

INTRODUCTION

Carving gourds with a single U-shaped wood gouge — generally referred to as "chip-carving" — can produce a variety of effects when stained. But simply adding a few more gouge widths and changing the timing of the staining process will greatly increase the number of patterns produced. All of the projects in this book are carved with a total of four gouge widths, and they utilize only one application of stain. The projects are arranged in order to introduce a new technique or to refine a skill. A trouble-shooting section and a list of tips and tricks are included to help the carver visualize and develop their own original patterns.

This small selection shows designs carved with four different gouge sizes.

Designs carved with a 1/4-inch gouge.

Chapter One
Getting Started

Choosing Gouges

Tool manufacturers use the term "sweep" to describe the tool profile, that is, the shape of the cutting edge of the gouge. The patterns in this book are carved with U-shaped wood gouges with tall straight sides, usually listed as a #11 sweep. In this numbering system, a #9 sweep would cut a semi-circle, and any lower number would be a flatter bowl-shaped cut.

Unfortunately there is no industry standard, so a good way to choose gouges is to go to a store that carries woodworking tools and actually look at the tools yourself. If possible take along a gourd so you can see the cut. Even better — attend a gourd show where carving is being taught or demonstrated! If you prefer to order tools from a catalog or the Internet, then look for a tool profile chart for that brand.

Similarly, the way the width of the gouge is measured may vary among manufacturers, depending on whether the measurement is taken from tip to tip of the gouge or part way up the actual cut (since the cut is not uniformly wide when the tool is used). A variation of a 1/16 of an inch will carve with a noticeable difference, and the four widths of gouges chosen for these projects are 1/16, 1/8, 3/16, and 1/4 inches. The 1/16 inch gouge is most useful for carving lines of a pleasing width — anything much smaller tends to bite more deeply and is difficult to move forward. The 1/8 inch is a good size for small gourds while the 3/16 inch is a better proportion for medium-sized gourds, especially if the pattern has a lot of twists and turns. The 1/4 inch gouge will produce the proper scale carving for large gourds. Looking at a ruler with both inches and millimeters marked side by side is an easy way to convert from English measurements to the metric system used by Swiss or German manufacturers.

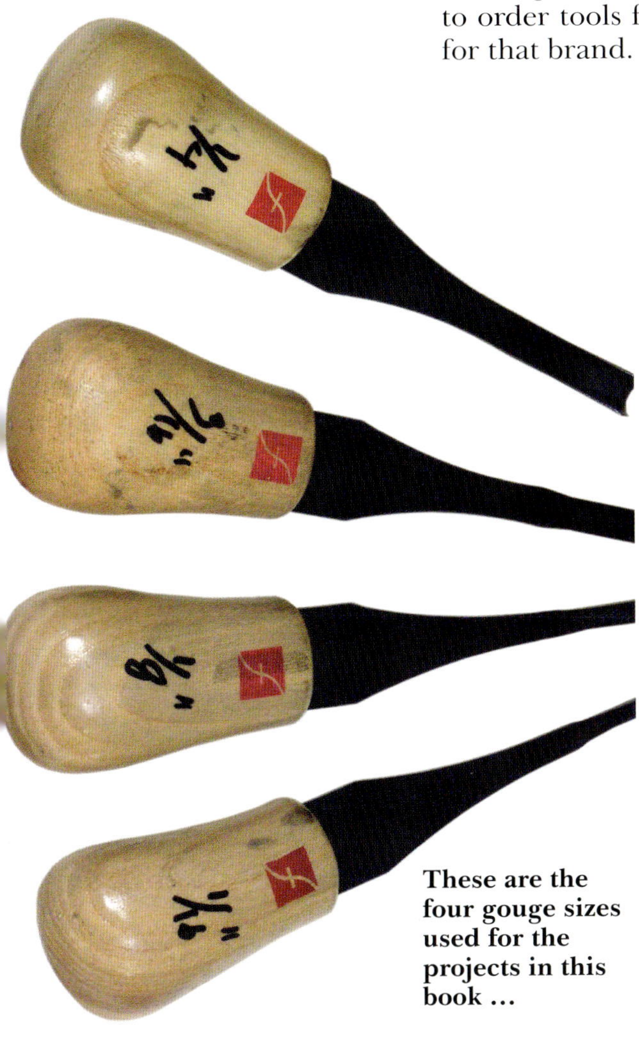

These are the four gouge sizes used for the projects in this book …

This carving was made by using these four gouges.

Handle shape is a matter of comfort. If you have not done enough carving to establish a preference, you may wish to try one of the gouge sizes and see if you are comfortable with the handle shape before investing in a whole set. Just a note of caution: "mini-gouges" with pencil-size handles may be adequate for a small amount of work, but are really hard to use for long periods of time because they force your hand into a tightly cramped position.

Handle length is not usually a problem, but choose a length that is comfortable so that your arm is not put at an awkward angle because of the combined length of the tool shaft and handle. Palm tools are often chosen for the comfort of their handles and they will work on gourds in almost all situations except for very tightly curved gourds where a short tool does not leave enough room for the hand.

Selecting Gourds

A good carving gourd will have a uniformly sturdy shell with a clear skin. If you are buying dry gourds, a gourd grown in the south or west where the growing season is longer will probably have a thicker shell, but northern gourds are also suitable once you develop a lighter touch. Beginning carvers tend to exert more pressure than necessary, and it is possible to carve so deeply that the gouge will go through the shell, especially on the smaller ornament size hardshell gourds. For first projects choose a gourd that feels heavy for its size; a sturdy stem is also an indication of a good shell for carving. Test the gourd by exerting pressure from your thumbs all over the gourd — there should be no "give" at all.

If you are cleaning dry gourds for carving, use warm soapy water and the back side of a table knife or a plastic kitchen scrubbie so that any outer skin is removed without leaving scratch marks that will interfere with the carved patterns. Scars and insect damage will stain dark and will show less if the carving on the gourds is done after staining, however dark mosaic patterns may actually be etched into the fibrous layer under the shell and should be avoided if the pattern depends on light colored carving.

Additional Tools and Supplies

Most of the patterns in this book are highlighted with one application of brown leather dye topped off with brown paste shoe polish. The staining process will be shown step by step in the first project. Alcohol-based leather dye is the product of choice simply because it dries so quickly, and can be easily tone-adjusted by adding rubbing alcohol. The shoe polish is used to darken the carving and bring a pleasant glow to the carved gourd.

Guidelines for carving and cutting are usually penciled on, and then erased before staining. A cloth measuring tape, compass with a sharp point, and stencils are used in some of the projects. Depending on the desired finish, some of the projects may be embellished with ribbon, beads, acrylic paint, or watercolors. Hardware stores and woodcarving supply houses sell the kits needed to complete the kaleidoscope, magnifier, and lighted projects.

Tools for cutting the gourds are a matter of individual preference. If you have a mini-jigsaw that you are comfortable using on gourds, it may be your tool of choice. But remember that you should be able to hold the gourd securely with one hand while operating any power tool since gourds are hard to put in a

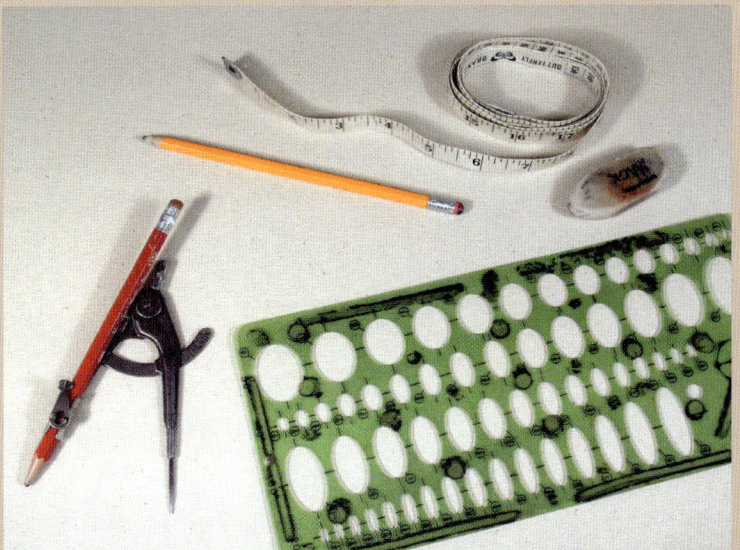

Measuring and marking tools. Compass, pencil, measuring tape, and flexible ruler for marking guidelines. Use an eraser to remove pencil lines before staining.

Various handle styles.

Keyhole saw for cutting, sandpaper strips for smoothing rims, and dust mask to be used while cutting and sanding.

vise. A safe, inexpensive alternative is a "keyhole saw" with a pointed tip that can be inserted directly into the gourd. Cutting and sanding is best done outdoors, and a dust mask or other dust collecting apparatus is recommended.

Many carvers use a Kevlar®, leather, or garden glove as protection for the non-carving hand and a non-slip cloth for steadying a gourd held in the lap. A sharp awl is useful for birdhouse construction. Wood putty to repair small holes and a pair of shears for trimming stems may also be helpful.

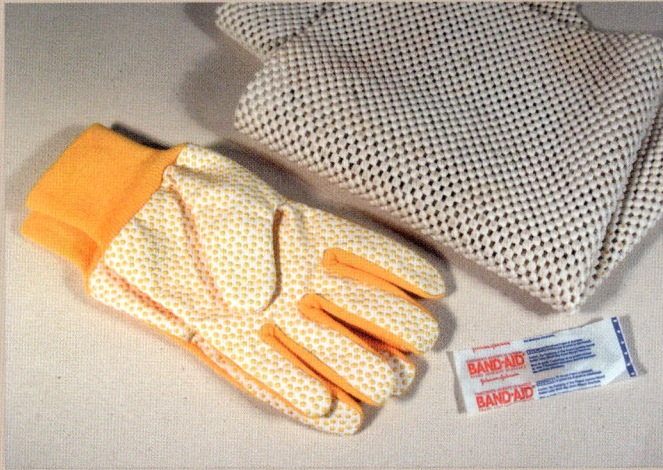

Safety glove and lap cloth ... hopefully the Band-Aids won't be necessary.

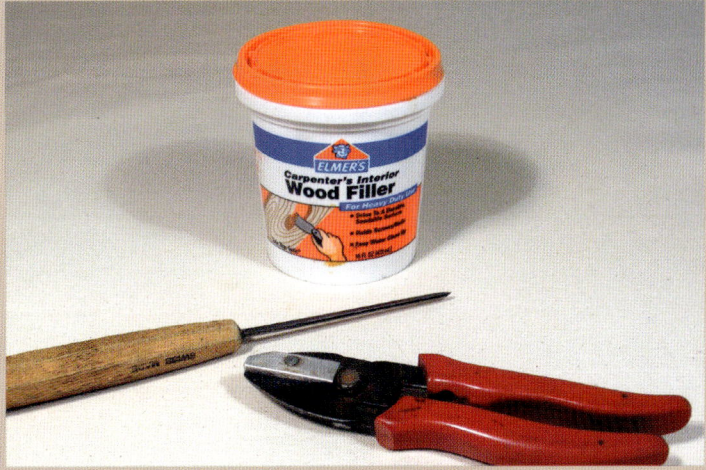

Awl for making holes, wood putty, and shears for clipping stems.

Chapter TWO
CARVING LINES

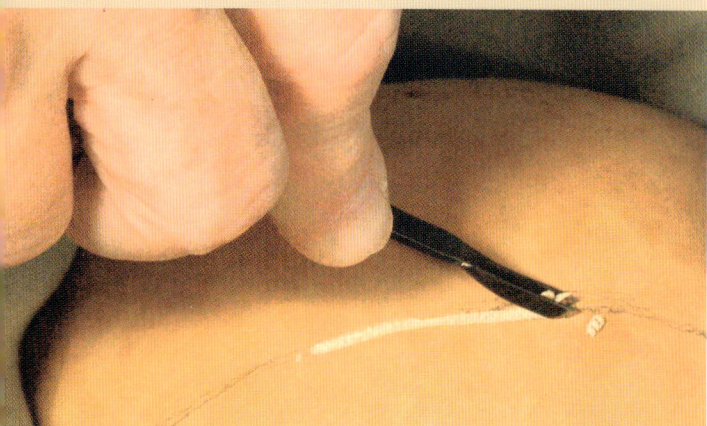

In classes, students often ask why carving lines is considered an advanced topic. The chips in a typical pattern are short and are easier to control. A larger size gouge used to make chips means that they will cover more gourd surface faster. In a chipped pattern, the lighter uncarved background stands out and less attention is focused on the individual chips, but with linework, the lines themselves are the pattern and variations in width and angle are more obvious. The curvature of the gourd requires that the angle of the gouge must be continuously adjusted to avoid carving too deep or you risk carving through the gourd shell — or too shallow, which may cause the gouge to slip off and scrape a trail across the gourd (or even worse, cut your holding hand).

However, since there are so many pretty patterns that use lines or combinations of lines and chips, developing a skill at line carving is of much interest to gourd carvers. This chapter has a series of projects arranged in an order that will help develop and expand your expertise at carving lines.

Triangle Bowl Pattern

A good first project to practice lines is this bowl with short line segments arranged in a triangular pattern. Choose a sturdy kettle gourd about 6 inches wide. Use a level line-drawing tool (or a pencil laid on top of a stack of books) to draw 3 lines. You will need a cut line for the top of the bowl, a line about 1/4 inch below the cut line to mark the tip of the triangles, and a line about 1 inch below the middle line for the bottom edge of the triangles.

It is much easier to hold a "bowl" as a whole gourd, so most often the carving is done before cutting. With a bowl project you can

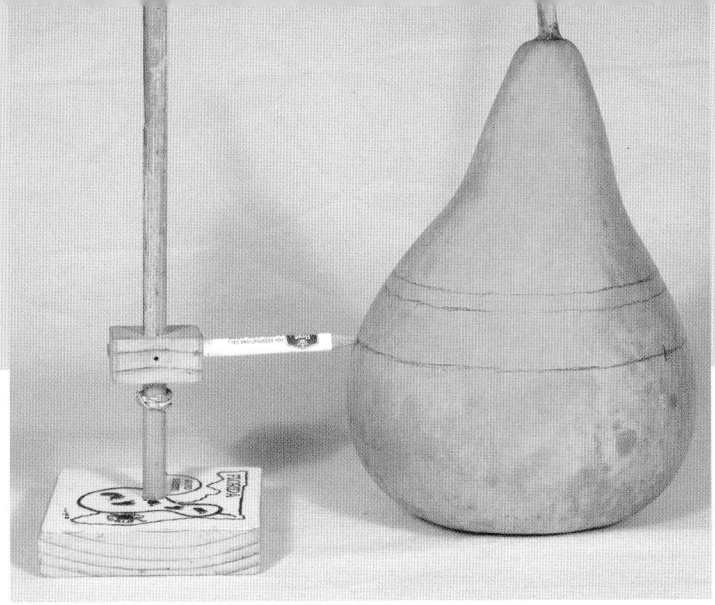

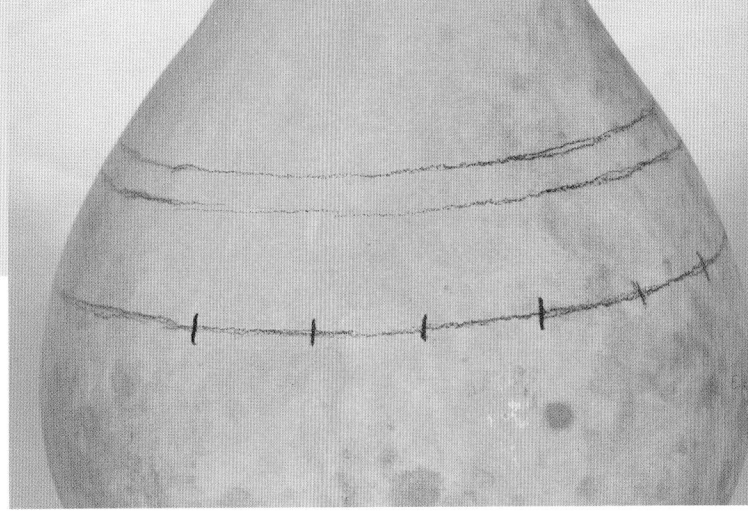

Mark the bottom of the triangle pattern with a level line drawing tool.

Space the marks 1-inch apart.

practice carving some line segments on the part of the gourd that will be cut off and discarded. Since there is variation in the hardness of the outer shells of gourds, a few practice cuts on the actual project bowl will be helpful. Shells that are too hard or too soft make carving uneven. With the 1/16 inch gouge held at about a 45-degree angle to the surface, a gentle rocking of the gouge should move it forward to cut a line. Practice makes perfect, but if the gourd you have chosen seems impossibly difficult, save that gourd for a different bowl project and try to find a more suitable gourd for carving.

When you are satisfied that the gourd will carve well, finish marking it for the triangle pattern. Make spacing marks about 1 inch apart on the bottom line, fudging a little to make the marks look even if necessary. You can wrap a cloth tape measure along the line to mark the spacing, but setting a compass length at an inch is a quicker way to make the marks. Draw freehand vertical lines upward from the spacing marks, and then draw in the diagonal lines to make the long sides of the triangles.

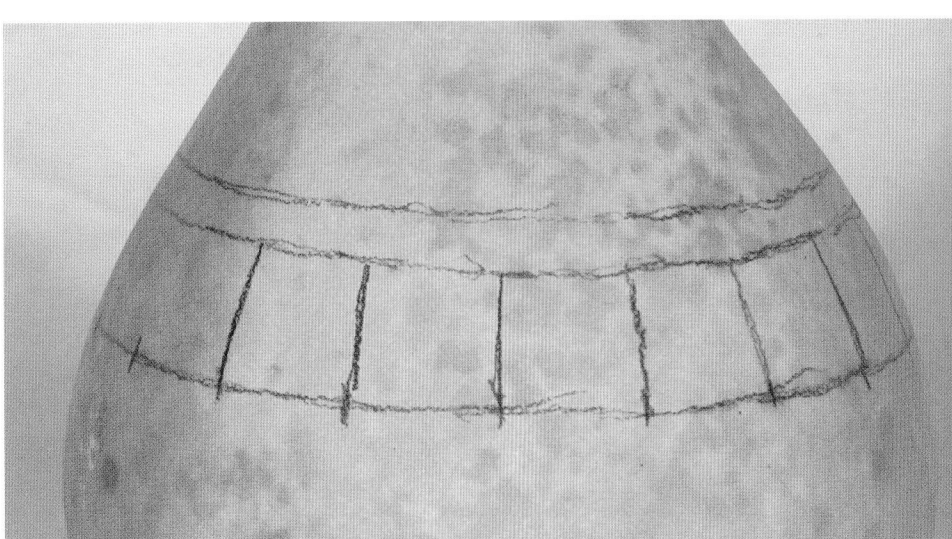

The vertical lines are drawn.

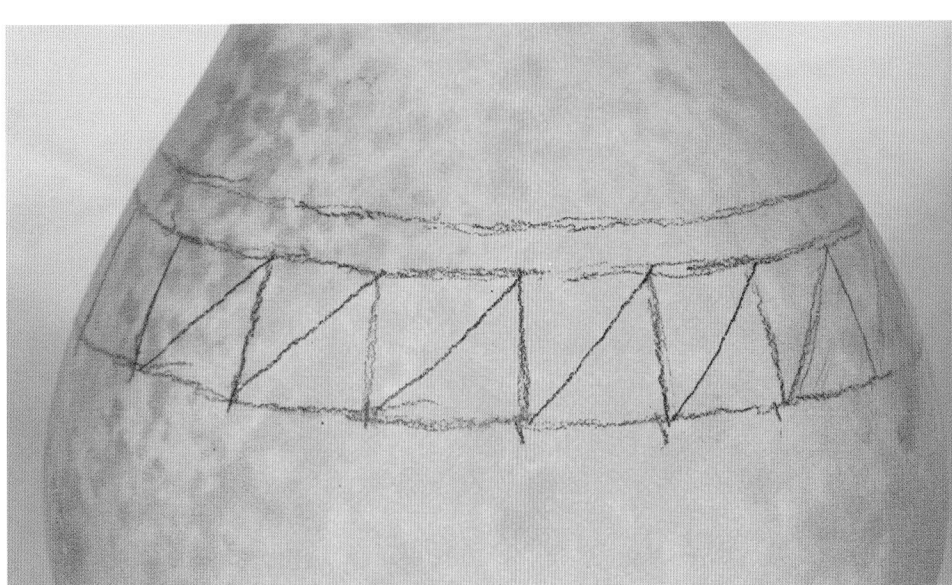

The diagonal lines are drawn.

11

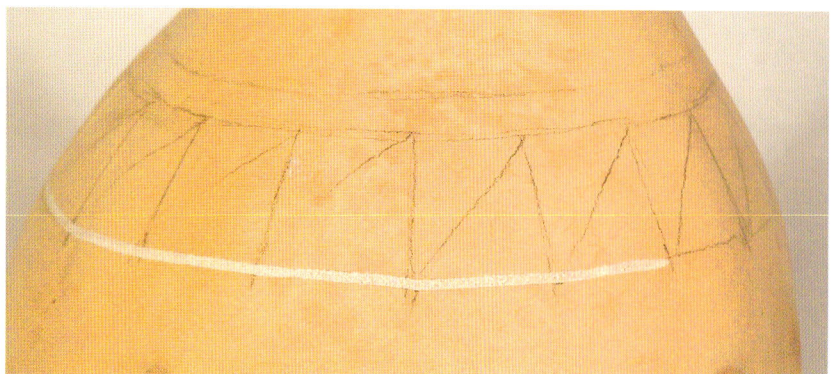

First line to carve...

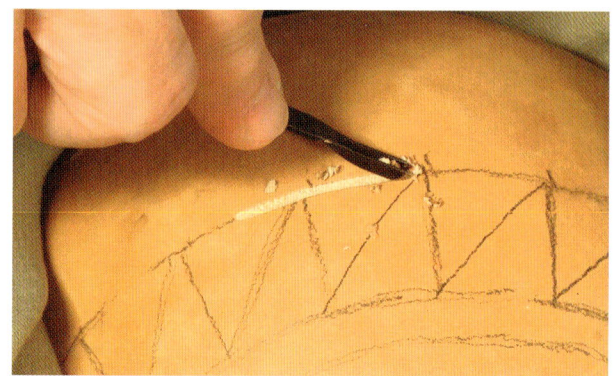

Only one or two segments are carved at a time.

First carve the bottom line using the 1/16 inch gouge. Because of the curvature of the gourd, it will be easier to carve in short segments. If you stop to turn the gourd where a vertical line will be, the unevenness where you stop and start again will not be as noticeable. Next carve the vertical lines; carving upward will give you practice at stopping on a pencil line, and carving downward will help you learn how to ease the pressure and slow down so that you don't carve "through" an existing carved line. Depending on the curvature of the gourd you may develop a preference for carving one way or the other. In either case, remember to position your non-carving hand out of the range of the gouge in the event it should slip.

Now carve one of the diagonal lines. If you penciled in some of the shorter diagonal lines inside the triangle, carve one — you may need to readjust the remaining lines because the thickness of the carved line is greater than the width of the pencil line. Don't try to pack the lines in too closely — three is plenty for each triangle of this size. After a few triangles, you should be able to carve the lines freehand, a skill that will save lots of time.

Erase any left-over pencil lines except for the cut line. Sometimes during staining the pencil cut line is rubbed off, but it can be added again. However, most often pencil lines will show through the stain and will mar the stain if erased afterward.

Now the bowl is ready to be stained, which will make all the carved lines appear darker than the background of the gourd. Although any stain for wood can be used, the alcohol-based leather dyes are easy to use and dry quickly. Leather dyes come in a rainbow of colors, but in keeping with a natural look and simple technique, just medium brown leather dye will be used for the projects in this book. (*Again since this is an open bowl, you can test the color on the part that will be discarded. The tone can be lightened by adding rubbing alcohol, or darkened by leaving it on the gourd longer.*)

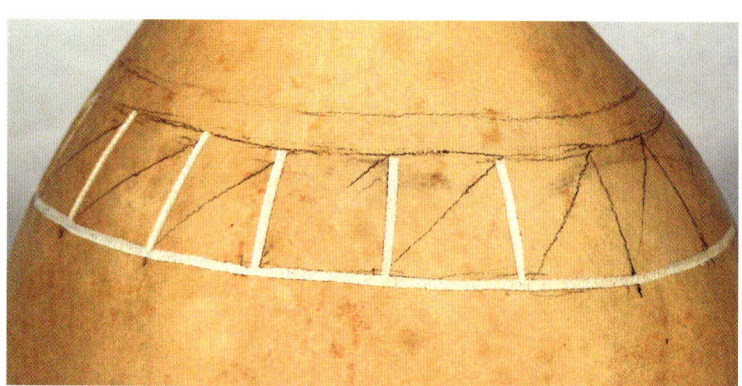

Carve the vertical lines.

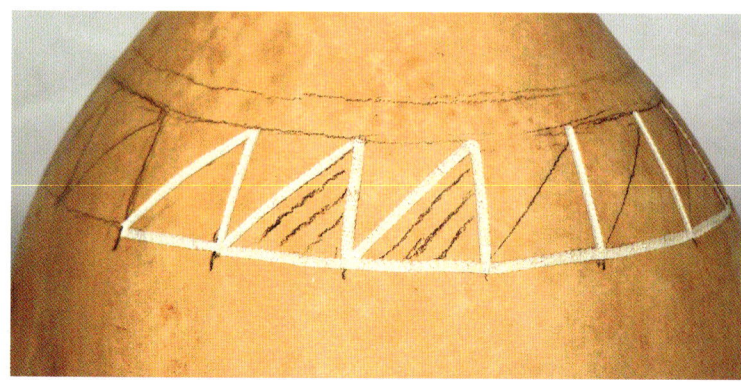

The diagonal lines are carved—pencil lines show where the remainder of the lines will be carved.

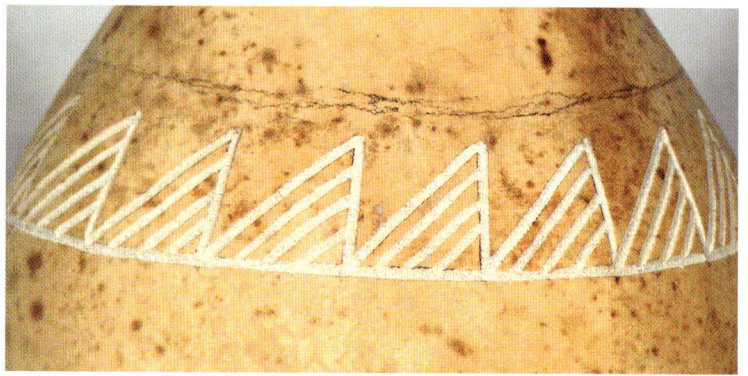

The carving is finished.

Cover the work area with newspapers and use rubber gloves to keep the stain off your hands. The daubers that come with the dye work well to apply it. Work on about 1/4 of the bowl at a time. The stain is very liquid and will soak into the carved areas quickly when rubbed with the dauber; the uncarved area does not have to be covered completely since blending the dye with a rag will spread it evenly. Continue staining around the gourd, blending well so there are no lap marks. Make sure the stain extends evenly above the cut line.

Applying a coat of brown paste shoe polish will darken the carving more than the background. A toothbrush works well for getting the polish into the carving. If there are large uncarved areas, a regular softer shoe polish brush can be used to apply the polish quickly. The entire gourd can be covered with shoe polish at one time and then buffed to a nice shine with a shoebrush or cloth.

Staining supplies: Leather dye comes with dauber applicators; rags for removing excess stain; and cotton balls and Q-tips for blending small areas. Alcohol can be added to the stain before application to lighten the color. It can be messy — wear disposable gloves.

Apply stain in small sections...

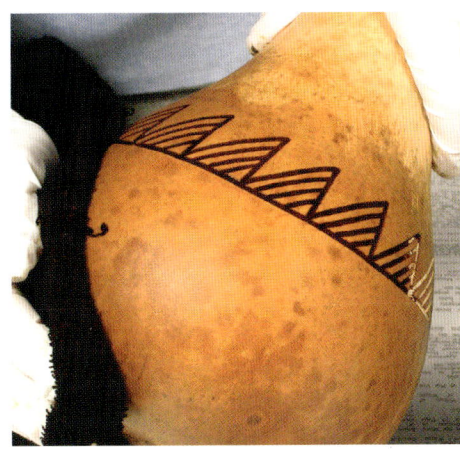

...and blend with a rag.

Polishing supplies: brown paste shoe polish applied with a toothbrush and buffed with a rag or shoe brush.

Brown shoe polish is applied with a toothbrush.

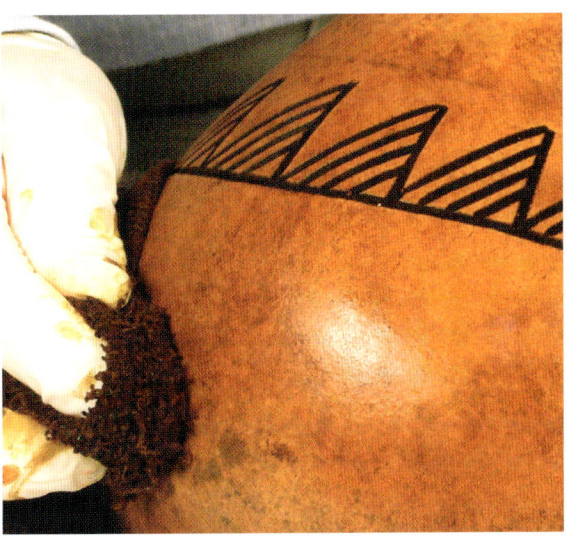

Buff with a rag or shoe brush.

Insert the point of the keyhole saw...

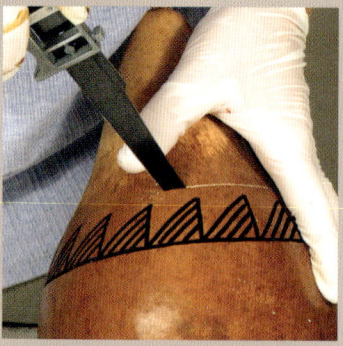

...cutting carefully on the pencil line.

Remove the seeds and papery material.

Sand the edge and interior.

Cut the gourd, and remove the seeds. Sand the edges and the inside. *(Don't forget to wear the dusk mask. Some people find the dust and/or any mold spores that might be inside the gourd very irritating.)*

Star Pattern Birdhouse

This project is also done on a 6 inch kettle, but will have longer lines and a more challenging pattern layout. It will also introduce the details for constructing birdhouses. Use a star stencil or paper cut-out to fit a series of 4-5 stars that just touch at the tips around the gourd. If you draw a line around the gourd where you think the top of the horizontal arms of the stars would look good and measure it with a tape measure or a piece of string, you can get an idea of how many stars of what size will fit. If you are just a little off, move the line up on the gourd to shorten it, or down some to lengthen it. You can also "cheat" a little by adjusting the length of the star arms in the back of the birdhouse. Size and number is your preference, except that the star for the birdhouse entrance needs to accommodate a hole an inch in diameter to make the birdhouse anatomically correct for a house wren.

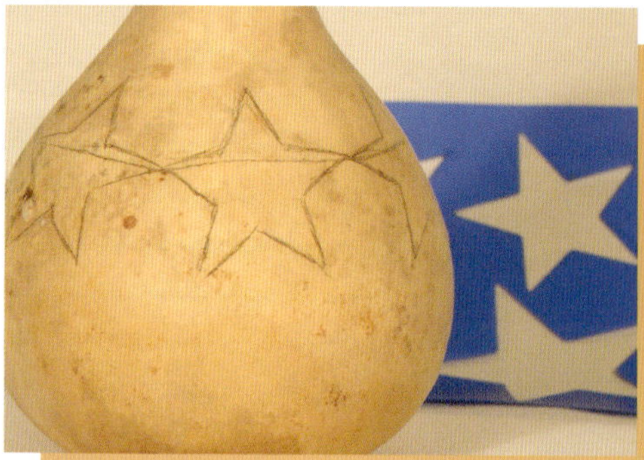

Stencil in the stars so that the arms will touch at the top.

14

Using the 1/16 inch gouge, carve the outlines of all the stars. Then carve a straight line from the top of one star to the next. Now carve parallel lines below this one freehand like you did on the triangle bowl. Continue along the top of all the stars, and then fill in the spaces at the bottom of the stars the same way.

Start carving the outline of the stars.

All the outlines are finished.

Connect the bottom points of two stars...

...and carve parallel lines freehand.

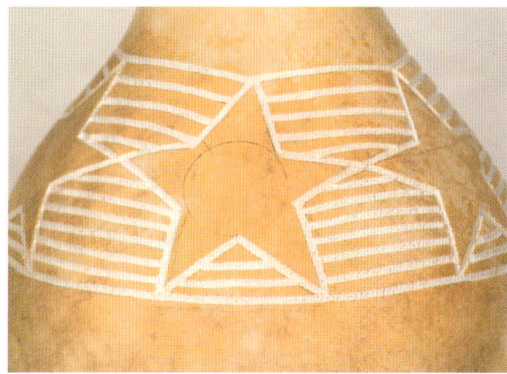

All of the carving is finished.

Choose a "front" for the birdhouse and draw around a quarter to make the right size hole. Use a saw to rough out the hole to within about 1/8 inch, and then sand to the pencil line with a strip of sandpaper around your finger. *(You can use a 1-inch hole saw or flange bit on a power drill so long as you can hold the gourd securely while using the power tool.)* Check for proper size — a quarter should just hang up in the hole. Use an awl or ice pick to make holes for hanging near the top and holes for ventilation in the bottom.

Draw around a quarter for the entrance hole.

Rough out the hole with the keyhole saw...

...and sandpaper up to the pencil line.

Check hole size.

Shake out the seeds.

Stain the inside rim of the hole...

... and the stem.

Use the same staining and polishing techniques as you did on the bowl. Apply dye to the inside rim of the hole and to the stem. The wax in the shoe polish will offer some rain protection for an outdoor birdhouse. Leather laces sold in shoe stores or craft departments of supermarkets make a nice hanging loop. Taping one end of the leather lace to a straightened out jumbo paper clip will make threading the lace through the hanging holes easier.

Thread a hanging loop.

Finished birdhouse

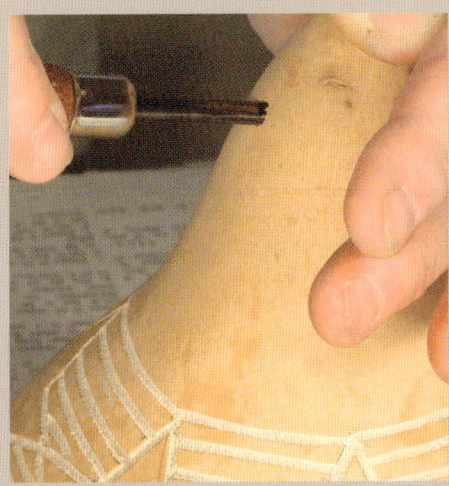
Use an awl or small gouge to make a hanging hole.

Make another hole on the other side...

...and ventilation holes in the bottom.

Basket Project

These perky little baskets are carved on cannonball gourds that are nicely rounded and measure about 4 inches across. The first challenge in this project is that the shells of cannonballs, while not particularly thick, can be rather hard. Also there is a much greater curvature to the surface of the cannonball, so slips are more likely. In addition, if a line is left unstained, the "white" line tends to look larger and more uneven than a stained line.

Begin by drawing a handle and a cut line for the basket. Add horizontal rows for the weave pattern stopping with a circle 2-3 inches in diameter on the bottom. Add vertical lines alternating between long and short — that will produce the little squares that will add the illusion of depth when carved. Carve all the lines with the 1/16 inch gouge. To carve the squares, just carve lines close enough together until all the shell is removed in the square. The "extra" lines down the middle of each splint are carved freehand.

Draw a handle and a cut line.

Next, draw guidelines for the weave pattern.

Draw more guidelines.

Stop with a circle on the bottom.

Carve the lines.

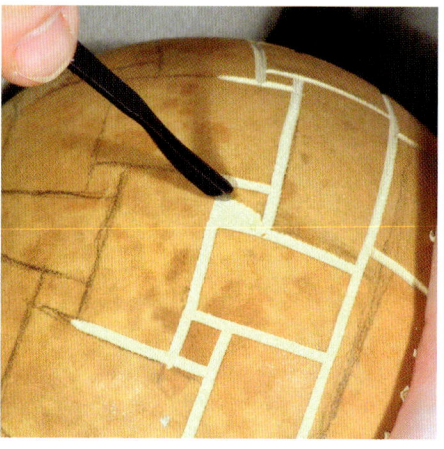

Begin to carve the "square."

The square is completely carved.

18

Cut around the handle and along the basket's edge carefully on each side. Shake out the seeds, and sand the edges and the inside. Once cut, if you decide you would like your basket stained dark, you will have to apply the stain carefully to get the color even to the edge without having the brown color seep onto the cut edge.

The basket can also be stained dark.

Cut above the carving and on either side of the handle.

If there is a small amount of stain on the rim, just sand it off, otherwise you can opt to stain the whole inside dark. Because the shell of cannonball gourds is thin and you are carving deeply, especially the little squares, stain from the outside may also seep into the inside of the basket causing dark spots. If you do not want to stain the inside dark to hide these spots — or any natural dark mold spots that are present in some gourd interiors — choose an off-white acrylic paint and coat the inside of the basket.

Here, the stain has seeped onto the rim...

Sand the rim...

...and the stain is removed.

Southwestern Pattern

As a final project composed of straight lines, this Southwest design is a versatile pattern that can be used on a whole gourd, a bowl, or a birdhouse. The kettle gourd in this example is about 7 inches across. Although the pattern looks intricate, you have already carved the "triangle" part and the "diamond" part is just eight repetitions of a small portion. Begin by dividing the gourd into four main sections by looking down on the gourd from the top. With the level line drawing tool, draw a line for the top and bottom of the pattern. The actual dimensions are not so important, but the pattern will look best if the top line and the bottom line are about the same length.

Visually divide the gourd into four sections.

In each of the four sections, beginning at the midpoints of the lines, draw a large diamond. Divide the two triangles on each side of the diamond into two rows of smaller triangles. Carve around all the triangles and add the inner parallel diagonal lines as you did in the first bowl pattern.

Draw top and bottom guidelines.

Mark diamonds…

…and side triangles, top and bottom.

Draw small triangles.

Carve the small triangles.

To begin carving the large diamond, pencil in four lines starting in the middle of each side and extending almost to the center of the diamond, dividing the diamond into four sections. Carve those four lines. The rest of the carving will be freehand

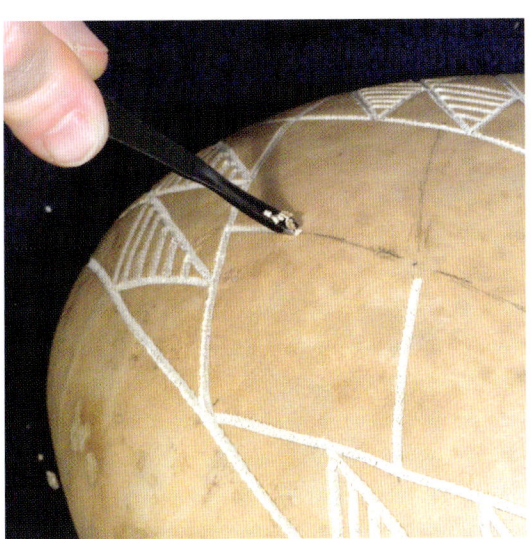

Carve four lines until they are almost to the center.

21

Now start at one of the diamond points and carve a line almost to the center of the diamond, dividing one of the four sections in half.

*Keeping the gouge in position at the end of this line turn the gourd and carve a line down to the outside edge of the diamond. (*The line you are carving will lie close to one of the first four lines you carved inside the diamond.*) Now go back to the center of the section and carve from the center down toward the outside of the diamond. You will end at the diamond border just to the side of the point. Slide the gouge backwards just a bit on the line you just carved, turn the gourd, and carve a line parallel to the diamond border. Slide the gouge back a bit on the line you just carved, turn the gourd, and carve another line. Repeat this turn-and-carve process until there is no more room.*

Divide each of these four sections in half.

Carve inside and parallel to the last line.

Fifth line...

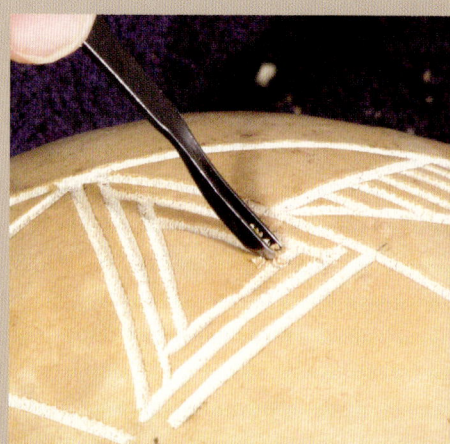

Sixth line...

The finished section.

Starting back at the center, carve lines, always turning the gourd in the same direction until there is no more room in the center.

Third line...

Fourth line...

Seventh line...

Eighth line...

Ninth line...

Repeat the whole sequence above *(in the section highlighted by astericks)* seven more times, and one whole diamond will be completed. Complete the rest of the triangles and diamonds. Stain and polish the gourd to make the lines stand out. Leave the gourds whole or cut for a bowl. If you want to make a birdhouse, draw around a quarter in the center of one of the diamonds. Add a second circle about 1/4 inch to the outside to make a nice border and then improvise the sequence of lines, which will stop at the outside circle.

Carve the remaining seven sections.

23

Again, same pattern... but on a taller gourd that has been cut as a bowl.

Here is the whole gourd ... carved and stained.

The same pattern is altered for use on a birdhouse.

CHAPTER THREE
COMBINING LINES AND CHIPS

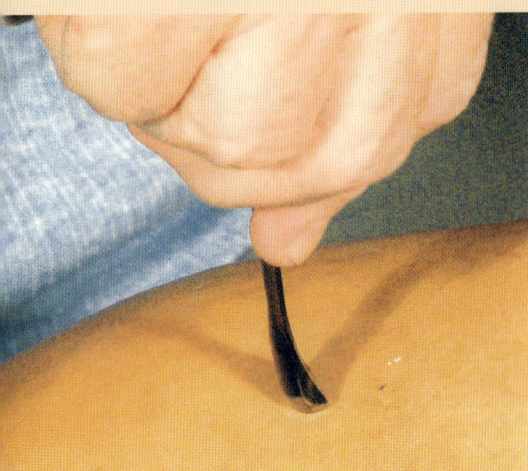

This is the hand position for making a stop cut.

If you haven't carved chips with a U-shaped gouge before, find a sturdy scrap gourd to practice on. It really is best if you use a whole gourd for practice since curved pieces of gourd are likely to break under the pressure of the gouge and are also much harder to hold with your non-carving hand out of the way if the gouge slips.

Start a practice chip with the 1/4 inch gouge just because it is easier to see what you are doing with a large gouge. Hold the gouge at right angles to the gourd surface. Wiggle it a little side-to-side while pushing it into the gourd surface until a thin U is cut into the surface — this is the "stop cut." Pull the gouge about 1/2 inch back from the stop cut, lower the angle of the gouge to the surface to about 45 degrees, push the gouge lightly into the surface, and move it forward with a slight wiggle of the wrist. Increase the pressure slightly until the gouge reaches the stop cut and the chip pops out. Practice until you can comfortably make a set of chips of varying lengths up to about 1 inch long. The same technique is used to make smaller width chips with the 3/16 inch and 1/8 inch gouges.

Make stop cut and slide gouge back to start chip...

...part way to stop cut.

Complete chip.

The stop cut is an important part of the chip. The tips of the stop cut that protrude above the chip will be used to "interlock" rows of carving to produce the swirl pattern characteristic of carving with U-shaped gouges. To convince yourself that the stop cuts will stain dark, look at the pattern inside the two stars — just stop cuts!

The pattern inside the star's outlines is made only of stop cuts.

25

Circular Pattern Birdhouses

Here's a nice little and simple birdhouse project to introduce using lines and chips in the same design. Draw around a quarter on a 6-inch kettle gourd. Using a compass with the point in the center of the entrance hole, draw a circle about 1/2 inch from the entrance hole circle. Draw a new circle to about 3/4 inch bigger. Divide all of the circles in half with a horizontal line through the center by drawing alongside a flexible ruler or a thin piece of cardboard. Divide the half circles with a vertical line. Divide each quarter circle in half with diagonal lines through the center point so that the band between the outer circles is divided into sixteenths.

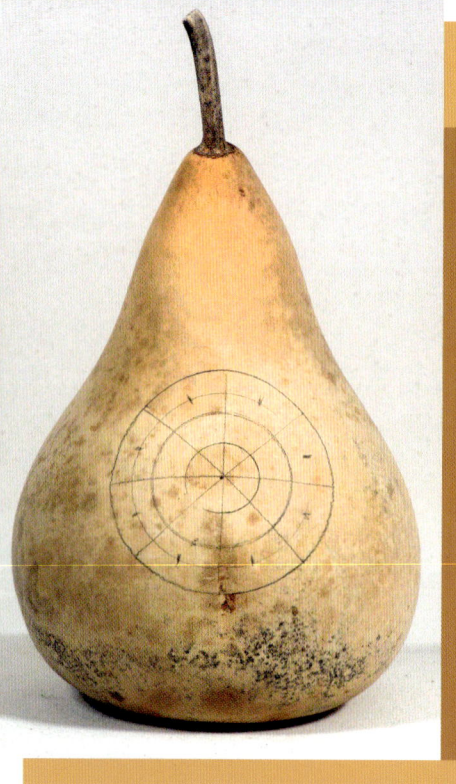

Mark the lines.

With the 1/16 inch gouge, carve on the line of the outside circle. This will be a longer "line" than in any of the projects so far. You will carve it in short arcs since you will have to turn the gourd often. Next carve the inner circle on the line. *(This will be harder to keep even since the curvature is greater, but staining the lines dark will smooth them out somewhat.)*

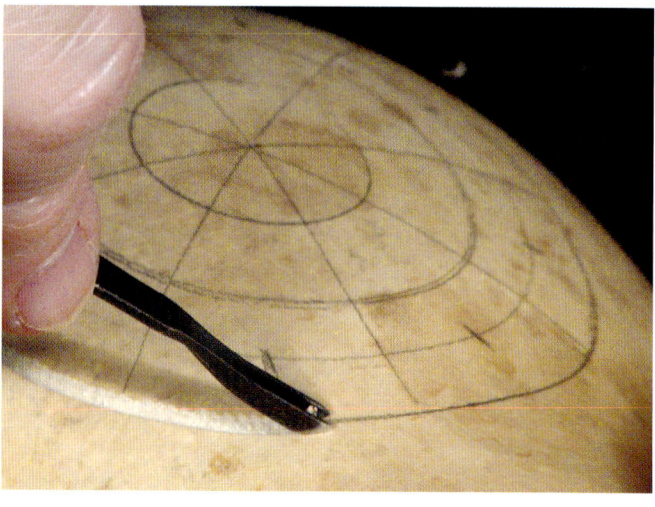

Carve a short arc of the outer circle.

To carve the pattern of chips inside the band, use the 3/16 inch gouge. Starting about 1/8 inch from the outer circle, make a stop cut on one of the spacing marks. Make each chip take up about half of the space left by the line behind it. Continue making the outer row of chips.

Carve the outer row of chips.

The inner row of chips is carved in the opposite direction. Make the tip of the stop cut for the new chip touch the tip of the stop cut of a chip in the outer row. This is called "interlocking the stop cuts" and is the secret to neat chip-carving.

Interlock the stop cut for the first chip of the inner row.

Carve the inner row of chips.

To set off this pattern, only the carved section will be stained dark. The two carved lines will keep the stain from spreading if the stain is applied with a small paint brush. Blend and blot with a Q-tip. Apply shoe polish to the whole gourd, and finish the birdhouse construction as before.

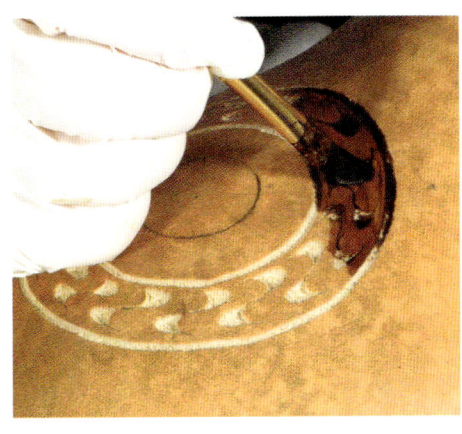 

Apply stain with a paintbrush.

Blot stain with a Q-tip.

Finished — see how the stop cuts are interlocked.

Here is a more complex circular design...

More Detailed Circular Pattern

This larger version of the pattern above is done on a kettle gourd that measures 8 inches across. The inner circle is drawn about 2 inches from the center of the birdhouse hole, and the outer circle is 3/4 inch larger. Divide the circles into sixteenths as before, but add an extra division line freehand to each section of the outer band to divide it into 32 pieces. Carve the lines with the 1/16 inch gouge and the chips between the two circles with the 3/16 inch gouge. These chips with their smaller size give a nice tight look to the carving inside the band.

Carve the rows of chips inside the inner circle with a 1/4-inch gouge to make a nice contrast. Four rows should fit nicely and give a pleasing blank border around the hole. If the cut line for the entrance hole does not look centered when the carving is finished, you can still adjust it before finishing the birdhouse. In this example, the entire birdhouse was stained with leather dye and then finished with shoe polish.

Use the same pattern layout, but with the circles farther from entrance hole.

The first row of the inside is being carved with a larger gouge.

Endless Circle Pattern

This elegant pattern, called the "Endless Circle," looks good on either a birdhouse or bowl. You can see that you already know how to carve the design elements from the last project. The key to pattern layout for this project is finding a nicely rounded bottle gourd and then fitting circles that just touch around the widest part of the gourd. In this particular example, the bottle is about 7 inches across and has 6 circles around the gourd, but the pattern is very flexible because you can vary the number of circles to fit. Start by drawing a line around the widest part of the gourd. You can measure with a tape measure and divide, or wrap a piece of string around the line and then fold the string into fourths, fifths, or sixths depending on the size you want the circles to be. Once you calculate the diameter of the circle that will look best, set the compass for half that distance and draw the circles with centers on the horizontal line so that they just touch at the edges on the line. If you are making a birdhouse, make the "front" circle in a pleasing position with regard to the overall shape of the gourd; if you're planning a bowl, it doesn't matter where you start.

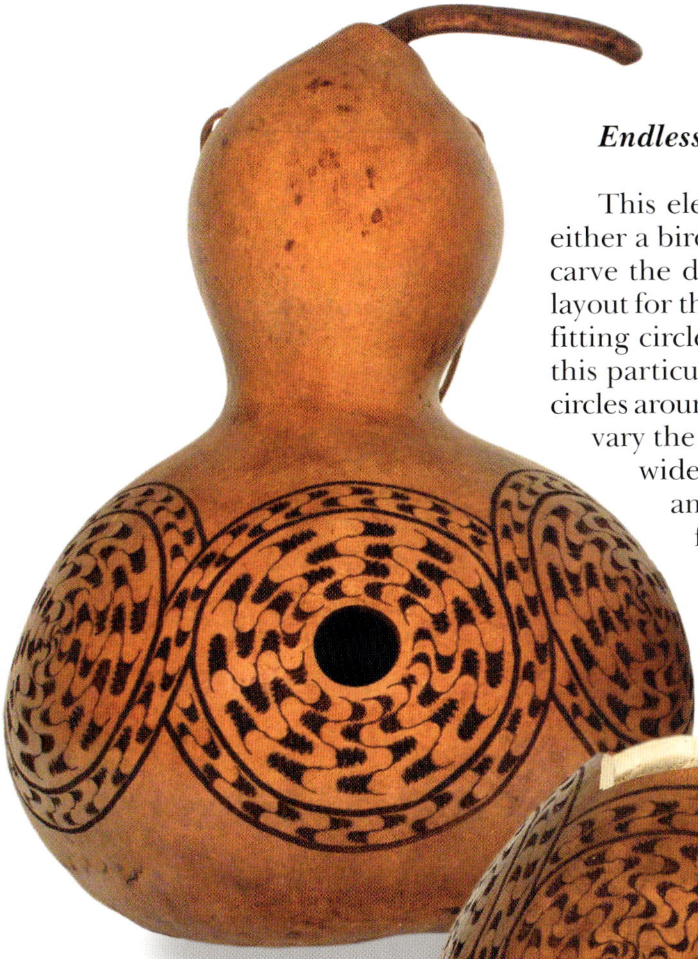

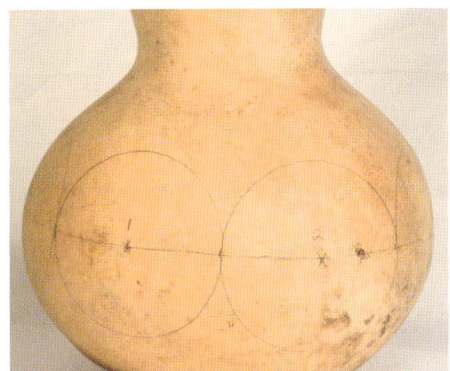

Guide circles should touch on the midline.

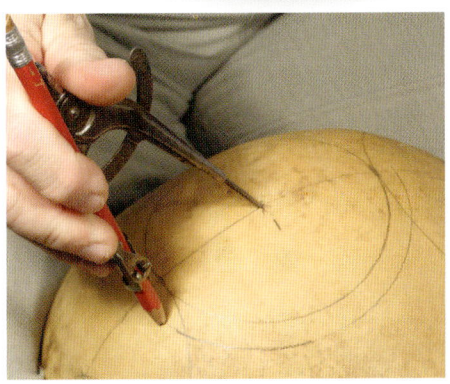

Mark the outer circle.

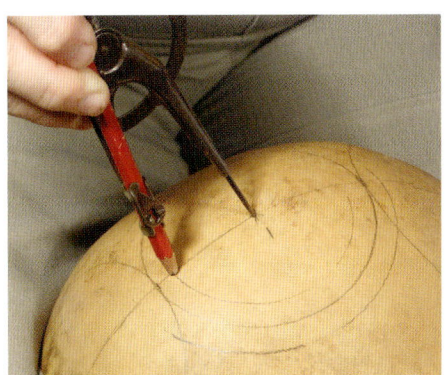

Mark the inside circle.

Erase lines to make the bands "overlap."

The circles you just drew will not actually be carved—it is the "centers" of these circles that are really important. With the compass point at the center of each circle, draw a circle about 1/4 inch above each original circle. Now go back and draw a circle about 1/4 inch below each of the original circles. Those two lines are the circles that will be carved — with the exception of the part of the bands that will be removed to make the bands appear to "weave." It is really helpful to erase the lines of the large circles to create the overlap before starting to carve so that you stop carving at the proper places on the larger circles — the inner circles are always carved as complete circles, and it may help to carve them first so that they look nice and round. It doesn't matter whether the bands lap "top over" or "top under" so long as you are consistent on any one gourd. If you look at the photo of the finished example, the birdhouse bands lap one direction and the bowl laps the other.

Draw the guidelines for carving inside the bands and circles.

You've carved the circles — the hard part finished!

Stain — note the centers of the bowl circles.

The only other new feature to this pattern is that on the bowl, as well as the circles without the entrance hole on the birdhouse, the carving goes all the way to the center of the circles. Sometimes there will not be room for every chip as the carving nears the circle center. Just leave out a chip at random when the space seems too small. It will not be noticeable in the overall pattern — look at the carving inside the circles on the bowl: there are only 5 or 6 chips in the center row.

CHAPTER FOUR
TWO-TONE CARVING

In all the projects so far, the leather dye has soaked quickly into the fibrous interior exposed by carving and darkened the lines and chips to contrast with the uncarved shell where the natural waxes keep the stain from being absorbed as rapidly. The interior of the gourd remains unstained under the shell, and if carving is done after staining, any new carving will appear light. Carving, staining, and then carving some more will result in two colors of carving for only one easy application of stain.

There are a few problems associated with carving after staining. The biggest drawback is that most of the carving must be done freehand. If guidelines are penciled onto the gourd after staining, they cannot be erased without marring the stain and polish. Some chalky marking pencils may be able to be removed (test first!), but will also rub off during the continual turning of the gourd during carving. In addition, after the routine application of the shoe polish that darkens the carving that is supposed to be dark, the surface of the gourd is slicker, and if the gouge slips, it will likely make a scrape that will be difficult to repair. Also those wonderful thin stop cut lines that show up so well after staining will be missing in the light carved areas. These factors taken together suggest that any light carving should be limited and kept simple for best effect. Of special interest for birdhouse makers is the extra caution that any light carving will not have the wax from the brown shoe polish as weather protection in the outdoors—and weathering will cause the light carving to darken over time.

Triangle Outline Bowl

This pattern is shown on a 6 inch kettle. Draw lines about 2 inches apart for the top and bottom lines of the triangles and add vertical lines at 2-inch intervals drawn up from the bottom line. Draw the diagonals and carve all the pencil lines with a 1/16 inch gouge.

31

Draw the guidelines...

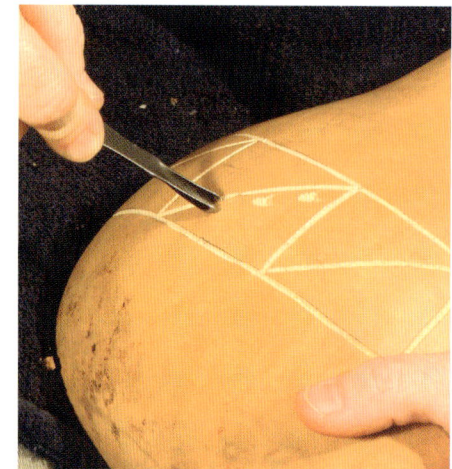
...and do the first row of chips.

This is the part of the carving that will be stained dark.

With a 3/16 inch gouge, carve a row of 4 evenly spaced chips along the lower side of one of the diagonal lines. Turn the gourd upside down and carve a second interlocking row. Continue alternating directions and leaving out chips as necessary until the triangle is filled. Carve all the triangles in the bottom row in the same way. Stain, polish, and cut for a bowl.

After a gourd is stained, the holding and turning of the gourd while carving will cause a little of the shoe polish to rub off — not enough to dull the shine of the gourd, but certainly enough to discolor your hands and clothing *(if you carve with the gourd in your lap)*. An old towel across your lap will do the trick, and if you do not routinely use a protective carving glove on your non-gouge hand, slip on a garden or work glove with a non-slip surface. Now carve the same pattern inside each of the blank triangles. On this bowl, the straight lines really define the pattern, and the carving is just filled in.

The bowl has been stained and cut.

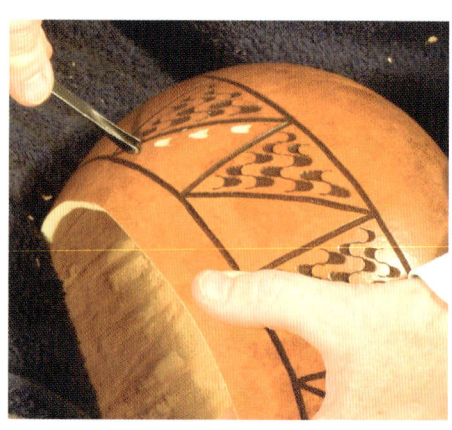
Do the first row of light chips...

...Finished.

Horizontal Bands

On a 6-inch wide kettle gourd, start by drawing a line for the bottom row of carving, a line where you think the carving should end at the top, and a cut line — these last two lines may be changed as the carving develops. *(In this example, the top and bottom lines are 2 ½ inches apart.)* Make spacing marks about 1 inch apart on the bottom line and begin carving chips with a 3/16 inch gouge for 5 alternating interlocked rows.

Draw the top and bottom guidelines...

...and space the marks 1-inch apart.

Draw vertical pencil lines to keep columns of chips even.

This section of the carving is finished.

Estimate the space needed for three rows of carving either by measuring or by laying the gouge profile against the gourd. Make a mark and then draw a level line around the gourd where the carving should resume. Begin carving more rows above the new line, making the first row face the same direction as the last row carved. The example has three rows, but you can easily vary the number of rows in the top band until it comes close to the guide line you originally drew for the top of the carving.

Erase all pencil marks, stain, polish, and cut the bowl. Now carve the lower row of chips, interlocking the stop cuts with the existing stop cuts. Even though there are no pencil guide lines for the size of the chips in this new row, you will see that the size of each chip is fixed since it has to fit in the space defined by the stop cuts. Carve the middle row in the opposite direction, and when you are ready for the top row of white carving, it will interlock with both the middle row of light carving and the row of dark chips above it.

The second example is a bigger bowl made from a kettle that is about 8 inches across, and the distance between the top and bottom lines is 3 inches. It is carved in essentially the same way except that a 1/4-inch gouge is used because it better fits the scale of the gourd. Space is left for 2 rows of carving this time, and note that for even rows of light carving, the top row of the bottom band and the bottom row of the top band should be carved in opposite directions.

Stain and cut for bowl.

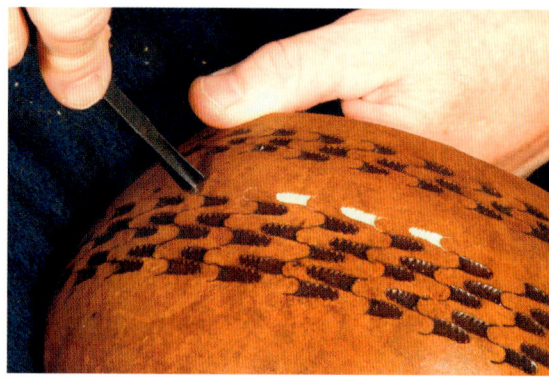

First row of light chips.

This bowl has a dark carving and space for only two rows of light chips.

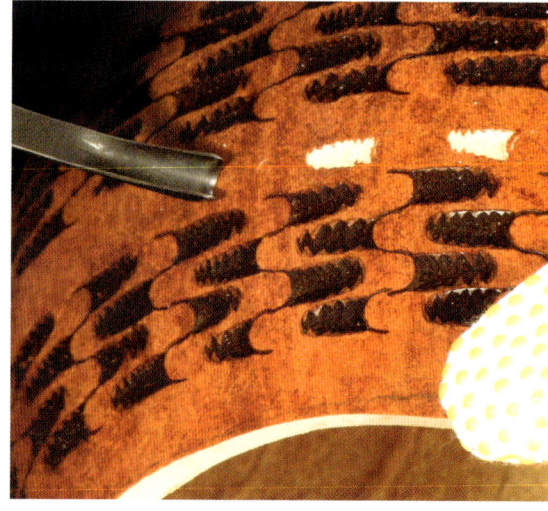

First row of light chips…

…the finished bowl.

Diagonal Bands

This project will help you develop a little more flexibility in free-hand light carving. This is a 5-inch kettle, with top and bottom guidelines about 2 inches apart. Also draw a horizontal line halfway between. Mark 1-inch intervals along the bottom line, making sure that you have an even number of spaces, and if not, adjust sizing until you do; otherwise you will not be able to alternate light and dark bands! Draw lines up to the top line. Starting at the top, draw a diagonal line through the middle line, extending to the bottom line.

Draw horizontal guidelines.

Draw vertical guidelines...

...and more diagonal guidelines.

Erase the extra guidelines.

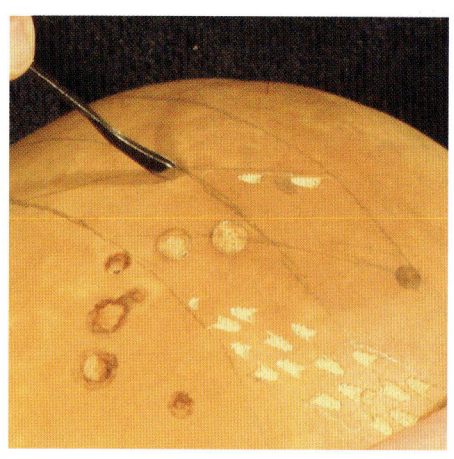

Carve chips along the diagonal lines.

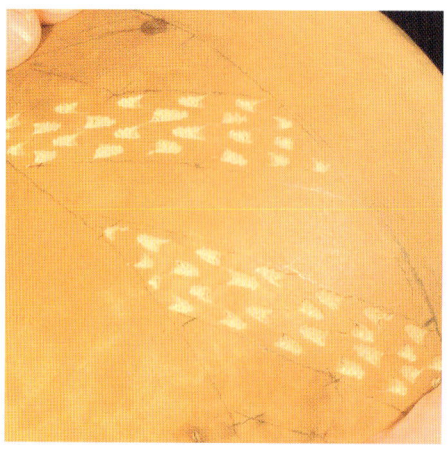

Skip a section.

Now, stain and cut.

Because this is a smaller gourd, this will be the first project carved with a 1/8 inch gouge to give a more delicate look. Starting along one of the diagonal lines, carve a row of about 8 evenly spaced chips top to bottom. Reverse direction and continue to carve interlocked rows until you have 4 rows. Skip an entire band (where the light band will be) and again carve four rows. Continue around the gourd. Erase the pencil lines, stain, polish, and cut for a bowl.

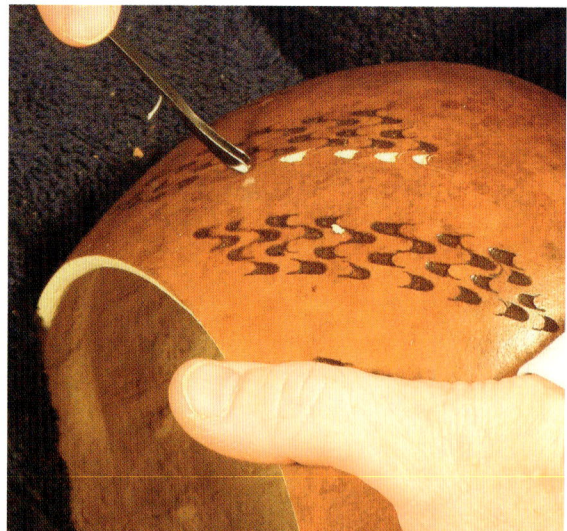

Add chips to the blank sections.

As you look at the stained bowl, if there is much slant to the gourd, you will see that there is slightly more space at the bottom of the blank bars than at the top. You will adjust for this by carving the first three rows as before. Then carve the fourth row interlocking with the adjoining dark row. Now fill in chips in the left-over space, interlocking chips on one side or the other and — most importantly — not stressing about the extra chips. They really will not show in the overall pattern where the eye will just be caught by the alternating stripes of light and dark carving.

Finished — look for the "extra" chips.

36

A New Fill Pattern

Now that you have used all sizes of gouges and have done some free-hand light carving, here is a very useful technique that will allow you to carve any geometric shape. The example here is a kettle gourd about 8 inches across with top and bottom horizontal lines about 5 inches apart and another line half way in between. You can choose the size of the diamonds to suit; these are about 2 ½ inches across, producing diamonds that are almost squares. Carve all the lines with a 1/16-inch gouge.

Draw the guidelines and diamonds.

Carve all the lines that form the diamonds.

In the middle of one of the top diamonds, use the 1/4-inch gouge to make 5 stop cuts that just touch in the center. Put a tiny chip behind each stop cut. Reverse the direction of the carving and make 5 slightly larger chips interlocked with the center chips. Make a third row, adding a chip when it looks like the space is big enough. Keep carving rows, alternating direction and interlocking stop cuts until you run out of space because of a line. Extend the carving with smaller chips into the points of the diamond. Carve all the diamonds in the top and bottom rows. Stain, polish, and then carve the same pattern inside each blank diamond.

Do five stop cuts in the center of the diamond.

Carve a small chip behind each stop cut.

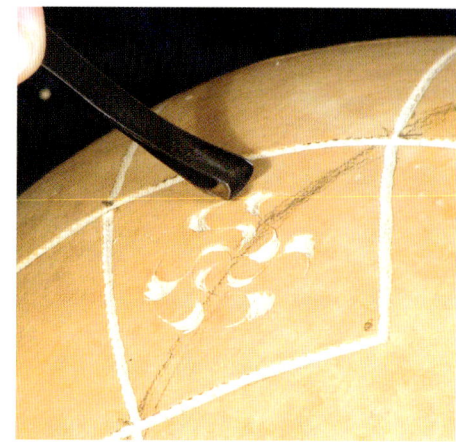
Carve the second row.

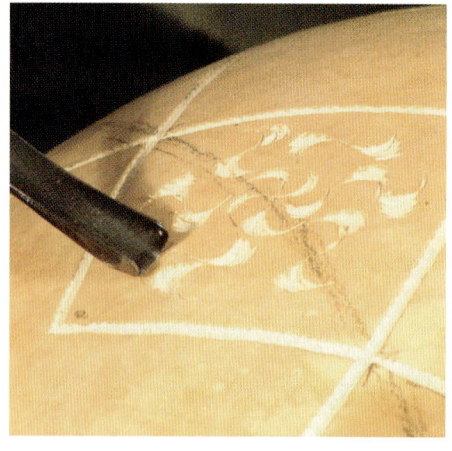
Carve more chips: interlock them if possible; add more if necessary.

Running out of space...

The diamond is finished.

All of the dark diamonds are finished.

Add light carving to the center row.

Diamonds are a gourd's best friend!

All-stars!

Depending on the size of the gourd you can vary the size of the gouge used to carve this pattern to fill diamonds of all sizes. This same technique works well on stars and the pentagons made by drawing lines between the points of stars.

CHAPTER FIVE
BEYOND BOWLS AND BIRDHOUSES

Getting tired of patterns for bowls and birdhouses? Besides being the two craft items most commonly associated with gourds, they are usually made from kettle gourds — one of the most easily obtained gourd shapes. The size range of kettles and the gentle slope of their sides also makes them ideal for practicing new techniques. However, in the photos of the various diamond and star patterns, you saw more variety in sizes and shapes, and this chapter will introduce some of those new shapes. You should now be able to look at these finished gourd projects and think to yourself how the patterns were laid out!

Vases

In general, gourds do not make good containers for wet materials. However people always seem to want gourd vases. Dry floral materials are fine in gourds although a large arrangement may require loose sand or marbles in the gourd to keep it from tipping. For short term use as a vase, wood carving supply stores (and sometimes florists) sell glass vase inserts to hold the water. Bottle gourds make nice vases because the flair of the top of the bottle makes a good edge to catch the lip of the insert. Holding the insert upright along the gourd will help you decide where to cut, but be sure to allow sufficient room in the neck of the gourd to accommodate the insert.

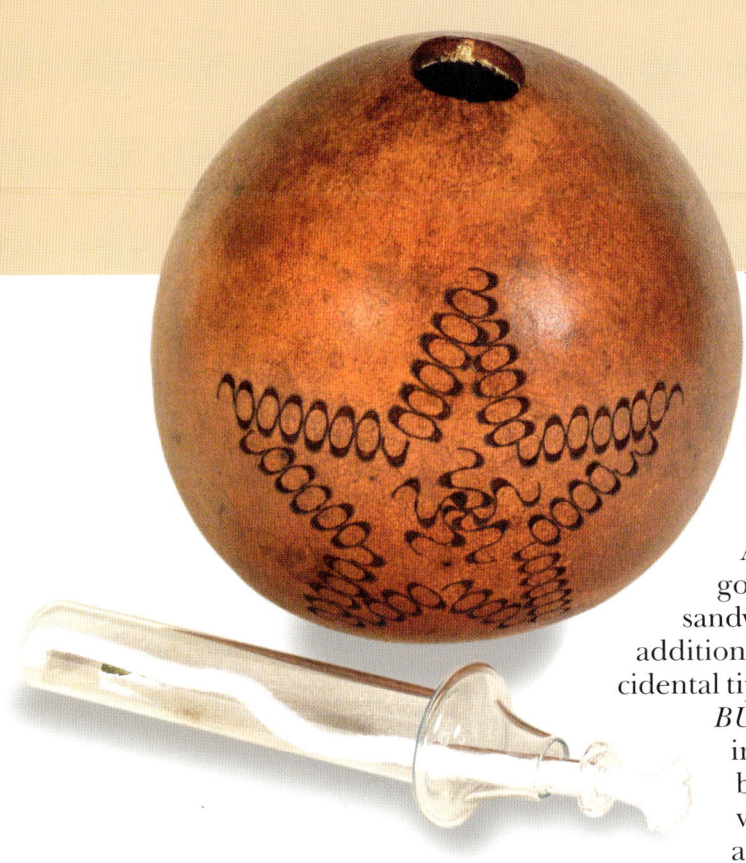

Insert oil lamp...

Oil Lamps

Use 4-inch wide cannonballs to make these little lamps — a fast-selling item at winter craft shows. Display the gourds with inserts in place, but remove the glass tubes before bagging them up for your customers. A card directing the user to "remove the insert from the gourd before filling" is helpful, and will fit inside a zip sandwich bag along with the bubble-wrapped tube and an additional baggie of sand to "stabilize the gourd to prevent accidental tipping while burning." *(It is also a good idea to add "NEVER BURN UNATTENDED" to the information card.)* The glass inserts with wicks are found in craft sores, and the end buyer supplies the scented oil to burn. Gourd "supply" vendors at major state gourd shows also carry these items and most of the kits shown below.

The carving on this star pattern is different — look closely and you will see that it is done by placing stop cuts with short chips across from each other around a penciled-on star outline. There is a short version of the fill pattern in the middle of the star. The snowflakes are done freehand except for the lines of the six arms; those lines don't show since they were carved off.

...finish oil lamps.

Magnifiers, Kaleidoscopes, & Mini-Lights

Woodcrafters who do a lot of turning are familiar with these kits from supply catalogs. These projects are fun to make, but do require precise measurements for the pieces to fit together properly. Electric drills can be used to put in the holes, but be extremely careful to hold the gourd securely since the stem ends and bottom ends of gourds are unusually thick. A keyhole saw may take a little more time and effort, but also gives good results, allowing the sanding of the hole to make a nice fit for the hardware.

If after your best efforts the hardware still won't fit, enlarge the bottom hole to accommodate a battery-powered "twinkling" candle. Use an awl to add some extra holes for the light to shine through.

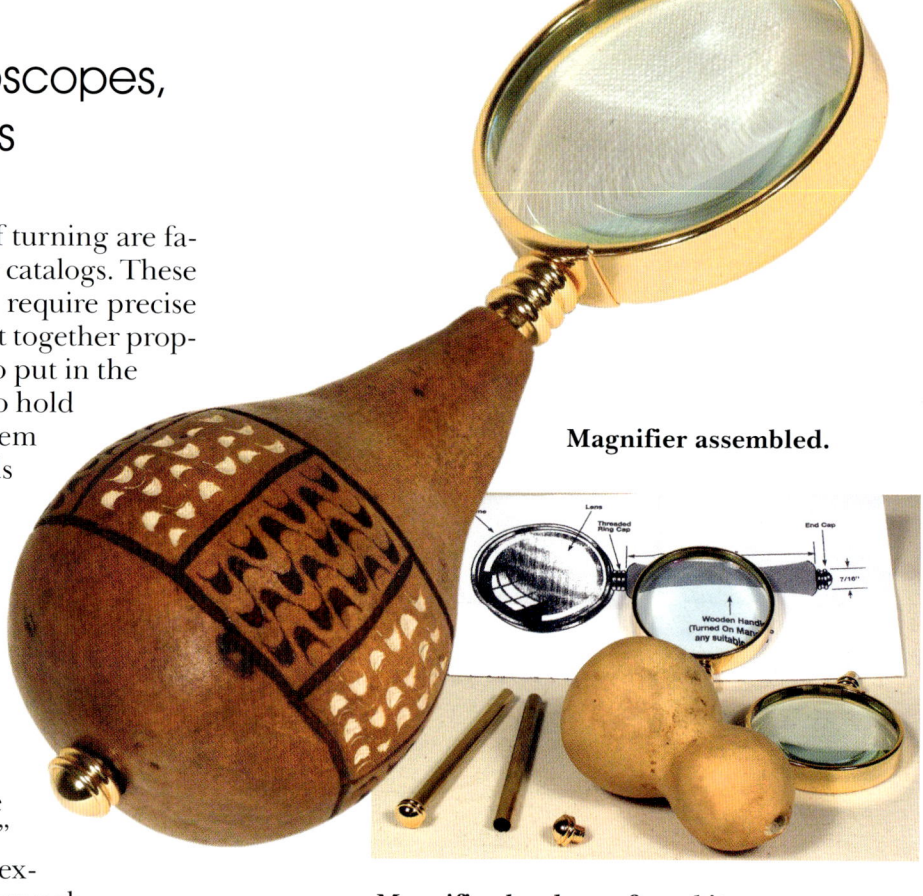

Magnifier assembled.

Magnifier hardware from kit.

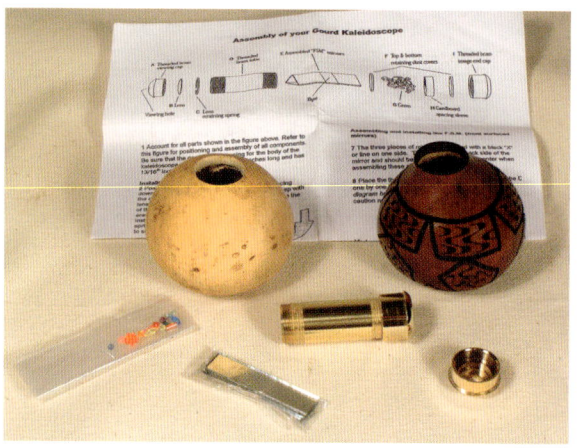

Kaleidoscope hardware from kit...

...kaleidoscopes assembled.

Battery powered mini-light from kit...

...mini-light assembled.

Jewelry!

Tiny gourds — actually named "jewelry gourds" — are sometimes sturdy enough to carve. If you're into jewelry, you will easily see how they can be incorporated into wearable art! The hardest part will be finding suitable small gourds — a gourd show with dry gourd vendors is the best source for these tiny gems.

Jewelry wire and beads...

...finished necklace.

Two-dimensional Ornaments

What can you do with all those tops you cut off to turn kettle gourds into bowls? What can you do with a beautiful gourd that has a crack or big blemish on one side? Make ornaments...

Tin cookie cutters make wonderful templates since the open side fits right up against the gourd for drawing around. A clip-art pattern was enlarged using a copier to make the bear template on thin cardboard. Ideas are endless!

In most cases, it's easier to carve the details of the patterns before cutting out the shapes. Exerting pressure from the gouge to carve a cut ornament may cause it to break because of the curvature of the ornament. A ribbon loop on the back makes a good hanger.

Some scrap gourds.

Cookie cutter templates

Stained gourd cutout ornaments

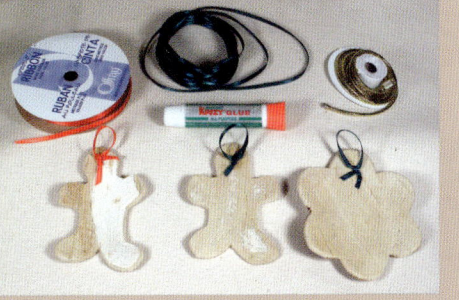

Ribbon attachments...

...finished ornaments.

Chapter six
TROUBLESHOOTING AND DESIGN

Since you have 4 different gouge sizes and lots of carving techniques, you are now ready to look at a gourd and analyze the possibilities for a good design based on the size, shape, and condition of the gourd. When other people find out that you "carve," they will give you gourds — gourds that you might not have selected as good candidates for carving.

Mold Mosaic

Consider these six canteen gourds with various degrees of black on the surface etched in from molding during the drying process. These gourds have been cleaned of the outer skin, so no more of the mold pattern can be removed. These canteen gourds measure about 7½ inches across and are about 4 inches wide. The stems will be left on for birdhouse "perches"; wrens don't need them, but people like them! Read on:

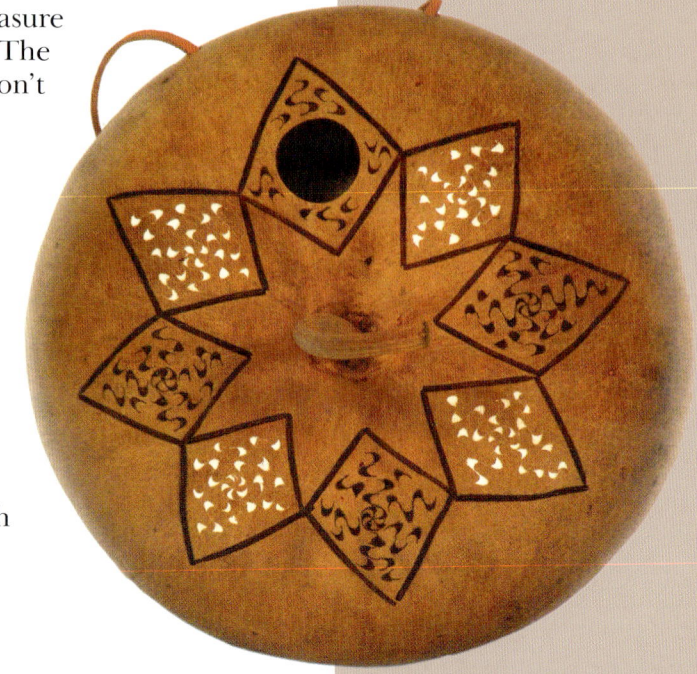

• The **top left gourd** definitely has the clearest shell and could be carved with almost any pattern. Both light and dark carvings will look good on this gourd, and the shell feels pretty firm, so the diamond pattern with alternating light and dark centers can be carved neatly. The fill pattern is done with a 1/8 inch gouge.

44

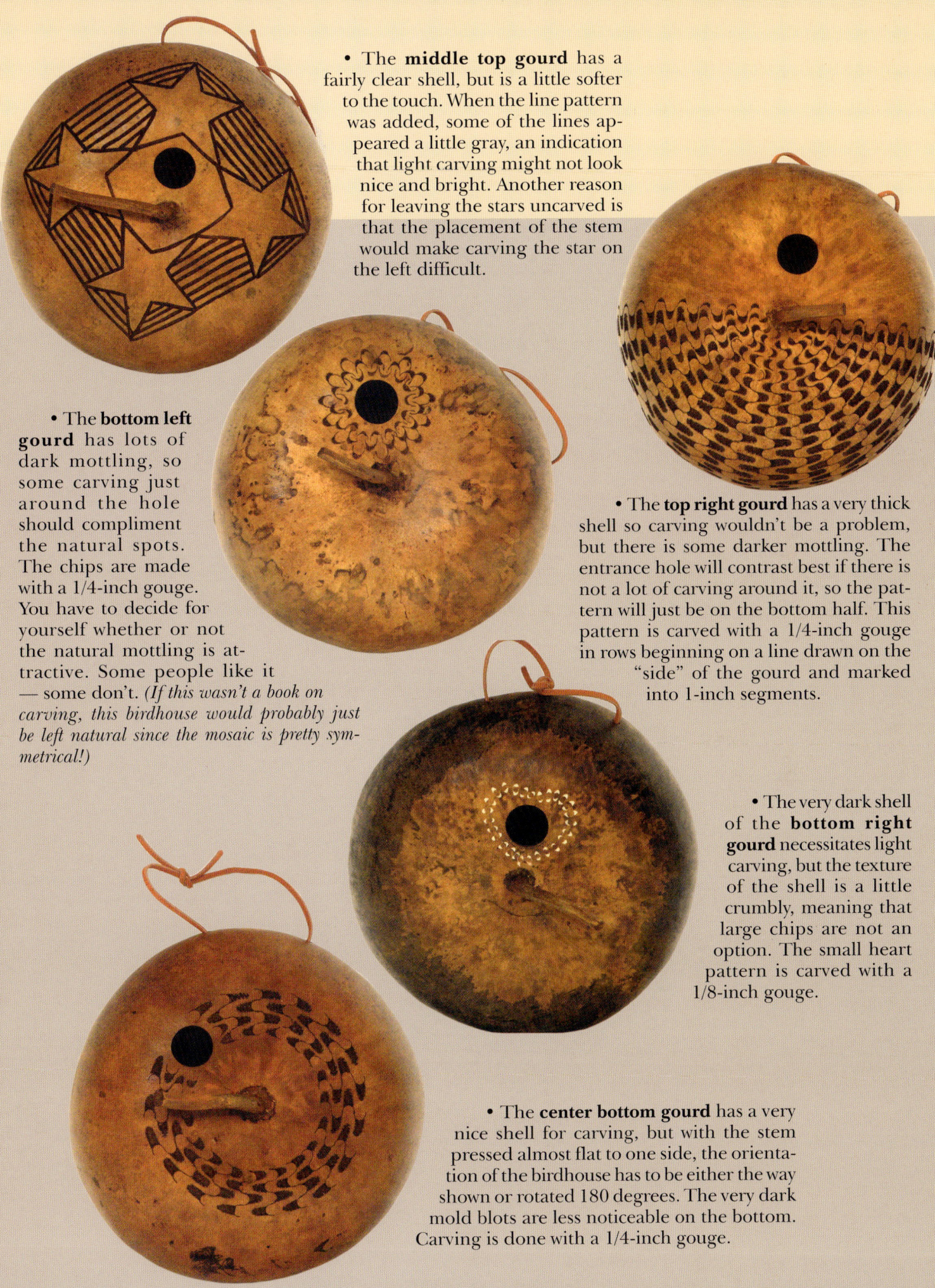

- The **middle top gourd** has a fairly clear shell, but is a little softer to the touch. When the line pattern was added, some of the lines appeared a little gray, an indication that light carving might not look nice and bright. Another reason for leaving the stars uncarved is that the placement of the stem would make carving the star on the left difficult.

- The **bottom left gourd** has lots of dark mottling, so some carving just around the hole should compliment the natural spots. The chips are made with a 1/4-inch gouge. You have to decide for yourself whether or not the natural mottling is attractive. Some people like it — some don't. *(If this wasn't a book on carving, this birdhouse would probably just be left natural since the mosaic is pretty symmetrical!)*

- The **top right gourd** has a very thick shell so carving wouldn't be a problem, but there is some darker mottling. The entrance hole will contrast best if there is not a lot of carving around it, so the pattern will just be on the bottom half. This pattern is carved with a 1/4-inch gouge in rows beginning on a line drawn on the "side" of the gourd and marked into 1-inch segments.

- The very dark shell of the **bottom right gourd** necessitates light carving, but the texture of the shell is a little crumbly, meaning that large chips are not an option. The small heart pattern is carved with a 1/8-inch gouge.

- The **center bottom gourd** has a very nice shell for carving, but with the stem pressed almost flat to one side, the orientation of the birdhouse has to be either the way shown or rotated 180 degrees. The very dark mold blots are less noticeable on the bottom. Carving is done with a 1/4-inch gouge.

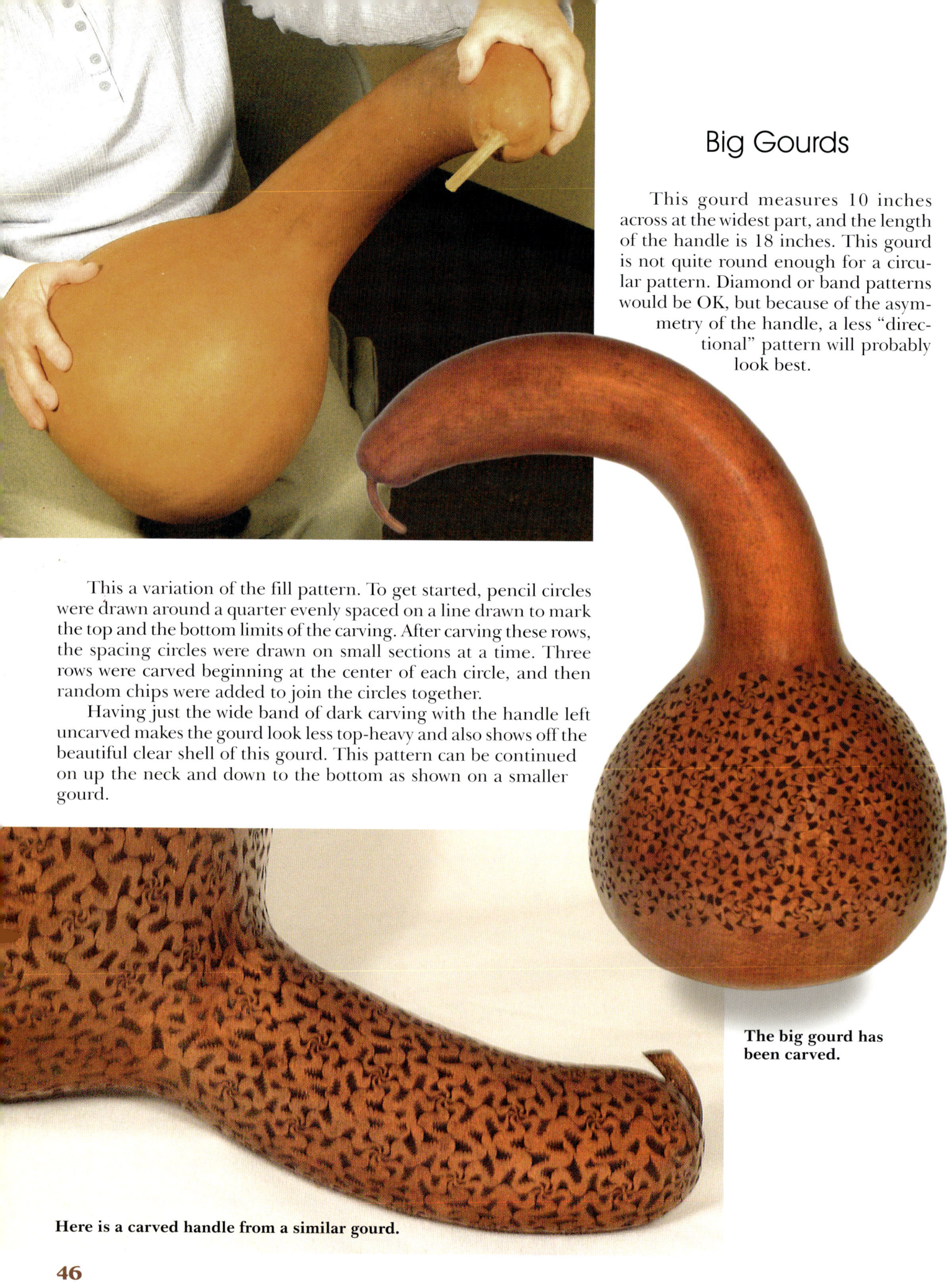

Big Gourds

This gourd measures 10 inches across at the widest part, and the length of the handle is 18 inches. This gourd is not quite round enough for a circular pattern. Diamond or band patterns would be OK, but because of the asymmetry of the handle, a less "directional" pattern will probably look best.

This a variation of the fill pattern. To get started, pencil circles were drawn around a quarter evenly spaced on a line drawn to mark the top and the bottom limits of the carving. After carving these rows, the spacing circles were drawn on small sections at a time. Three rows were carved beginning at the center of each circle, and then random chips were added to join the circles together.

Having just the wide band of dark carving with the handle left uncarved makes the gourd look less top-heavy and also shows off the beautiful clear shell of this gourd. This pattern can be continued on up the neck and down to the bottom as shown on a smaller gourd.

The big gourd has been carved.

Here is a carved handle from a similar gourd.

Long Gourds

This unusual dipper measures about 5 feet long. It was grown on a trellis to keep the handle straight, and was wrapped with rope in a spiral direction to make the indentations that give the illusion of a twist to the handle. The design for this birdhouse is three rows of carving, which follow the middle of the "twist" down the handle and then spiral around the entrance hole. Carving is done with a 1/4-inch gouge. The challenging part is keeping the gourd held securely so that the gouge doesn't slip off the narrow handle while balancing one end of the gourd on a chair with pillows to relieve stress on the long handle.

Whole dipper birdhouse

This is the same gourd...note the detail of the carving.

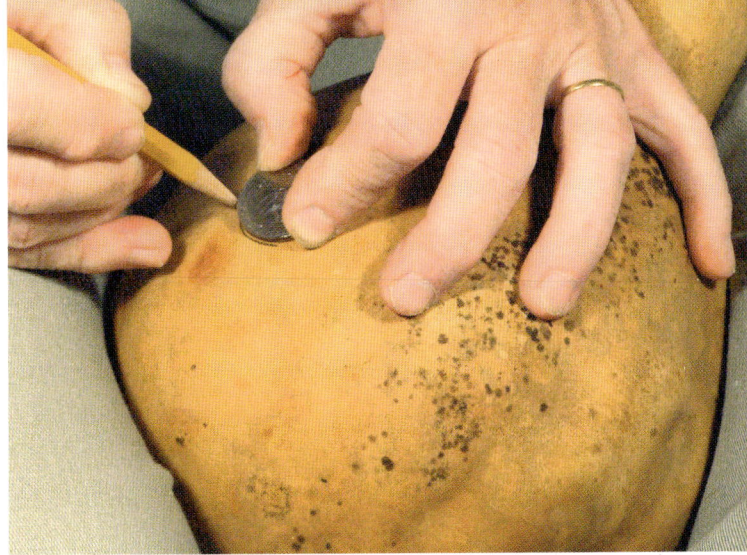

This is the bottom part of a long dipper.

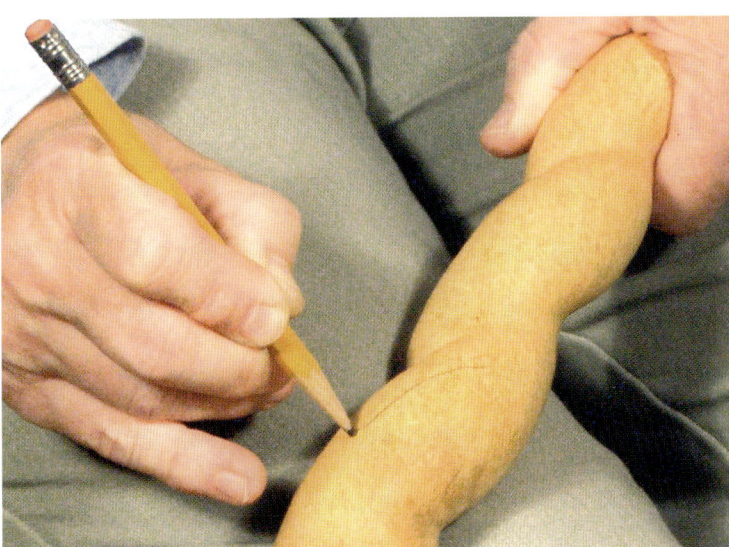

Draw the guideline for carving handle...

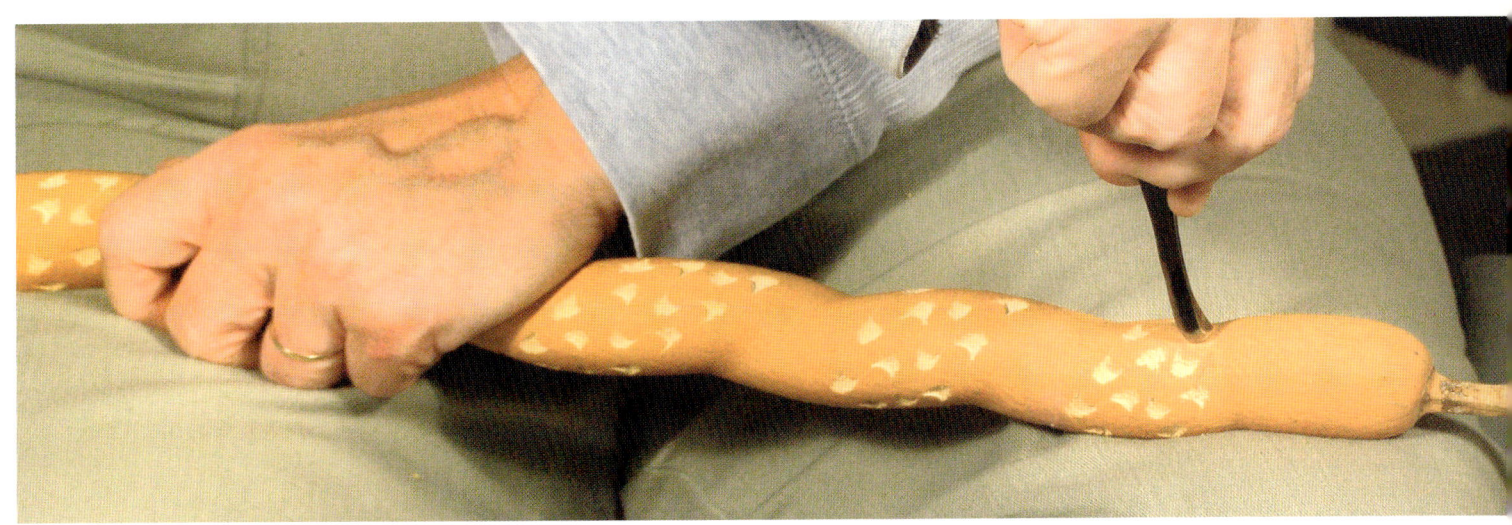

...and carving up to the tip.

Tiny Gourds

The two small gourds are only about 1-inch long and the third gourd is just slightly bigger. The challenge is to make a matched set of jewelry. There is not enough room for much of a pattern, so a simple swirl for the earrings and three rows of a fill pattern sets off the nice light shells of these gourds. The carving is done with a 1/8-inch gouge.

Jewelry gourds

Necklace and earrings

48

A Pre-cut Basket

A friend designed this basket *(made from a large jug-shaped gourd)* with a three-part handle and a diamond pattern and then was hesitant to carve it. It would have been easier to carve before the handle was cut since the gourd had to be held carefully to avoid putting pressure on the handle as well as the edges of the basket during carving. The size and shape of the basket made it very awkward to hold!

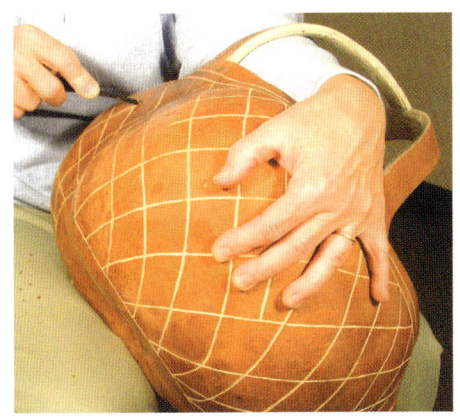

A REALLY…

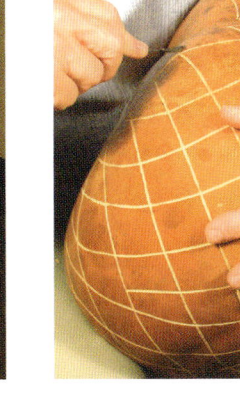

…big …

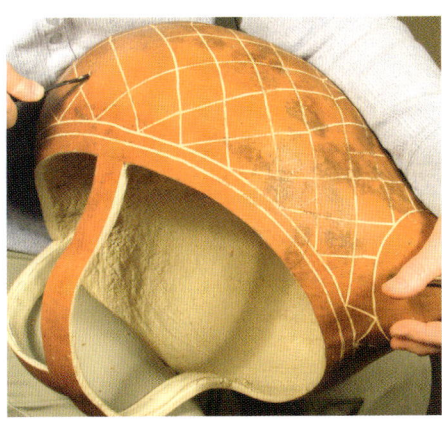

…awkward-to-hold …

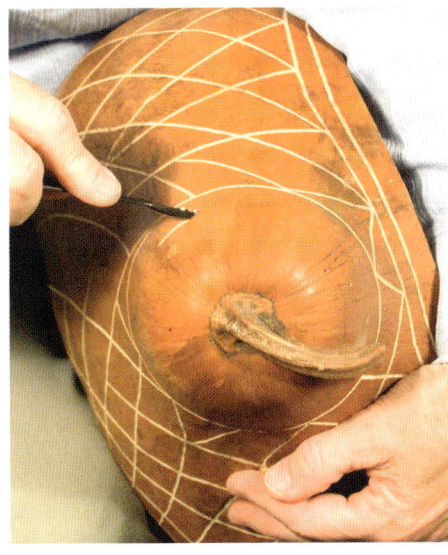

…pre-cut …

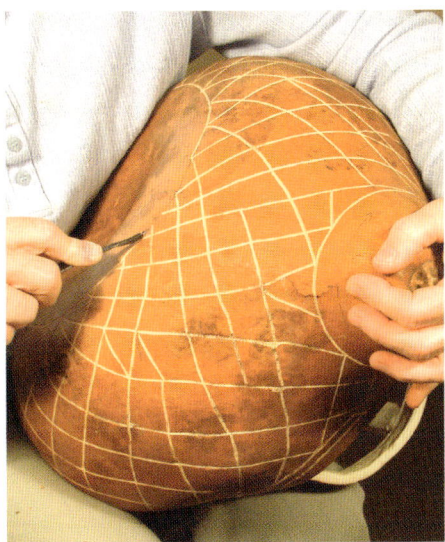

…basket …

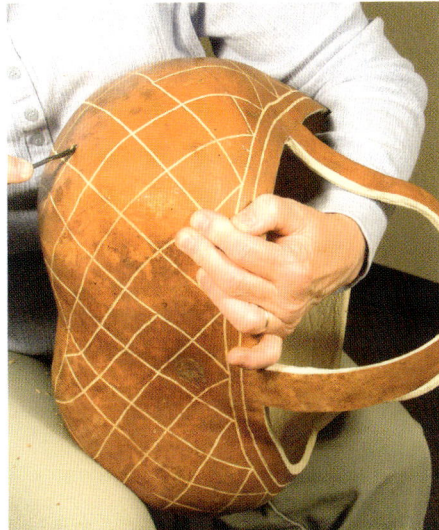

…gourd.

The surface has been damaged by mold...

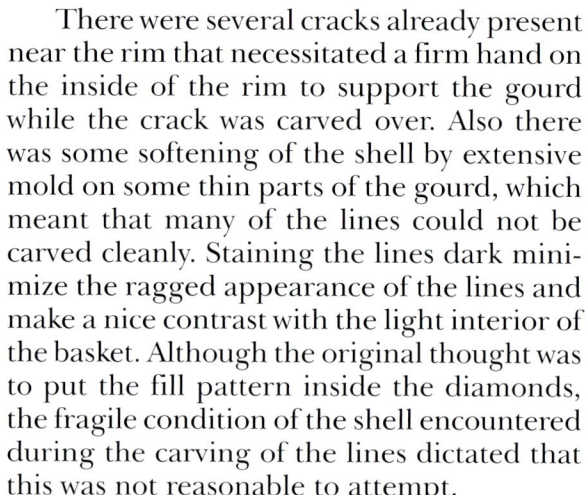

...and cracks are visible after staining.

There were several cracks already present near the rim that necessitated a firm hand on the inside of the rim to support the gourd while the crack was carved over. Also there was some softening of the shell by extensive mold on some thin parts of the gourd, which meant that many of the lines could not be carved cleanly. Staining the lines dark minimize the ragged appearance of the lines and make a nice contrast with the light interior of the basket. Although the original thought was to put the fill pattern inside the diamonds, the fragile condition of the shell encountered during the carving of the lines dictated that this was not reasonable to attempt.

Basket finished!

Chapter Seven
Tips and Tricks

This section addresses the most frequently asked questions during classes and at carving demonstrations.

Q: How do you sharpen gouges?

A: Run the gouge back and forth on a sharpening stone. Be sure to rotate the gouge as you sharpen it so that the whole cutting surface comes into contact with the sharpening stone.

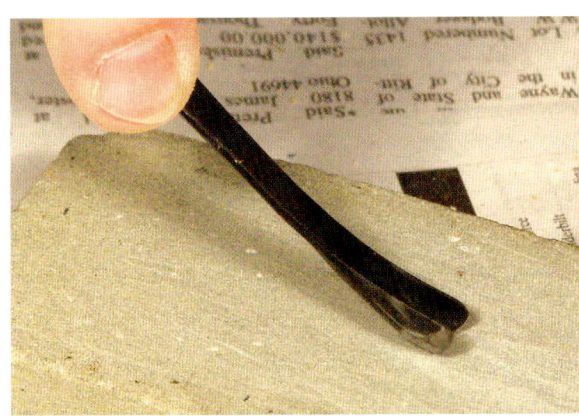

Sharpening stone

Q: I already have a set of wood gouges. Can I use them?

A: Yes, if there are U-shaped gouges with a fairly steep U shape. If the tool profile is a more bowl-shaped U, the carving will look different. A straight edge skew tool can be pulled along the gourd surface to make a very fine line — not much application in the chip-carved patterns, but it has some use if you plan to do some relief carving, too. This tool can also be skittered along the surface of the gourd to make an interesting succession of interconnected fine lines.

Flat gouge (top); shallow U-gouge (bottom)

This carving was made using a flat U-gouge.

Apply the flat gouge on the whiskers and "fur"...

51

Q: If I don't want to buy all four different size gouges, what two would you recommend?

A: If you want to do any lines, you need a 1/16-inch or smaller width gouge — sometimes called a "veiner." Line work really expands the kinds of patterns you can carve. Then your choice of gouge would depend on the size of the gourds you want to carve. If you're going to carve tiny gourds, you will need a 1/8-inch gouge; for most birdhouse size gourds you will want a 1/4-inch gouge. The 3/16 inch gouge is really a luxury item: you can make do with a 1/4 inch or a 1/8 inch, but the 3/16 inch just lets you get a few more chips in a given amount of space for a pattern with tight curves, making them look neater.

Q: What about one handle with interchangeable tips?

A: If you can get the individual tool profiles you want, this can be economical. There are two main styles of attachments: one with a collet, which must be loosened and then tightened to change tips, and the other — easier to use — with tips that slide right into the handle.

Here are some interchangeable tips.

Q: The stem broke off of a gourd I want to use. How can I fix it?

A: If you have the original stem, just secure it with a drop of super glue. Each time you cut off the top of a gourd to make a bowl, save those stems as replacements for lost stems. Most stems are wider at the base: look at the depression in the gourd where the stem is missing and cut a piece of replacement stem to fit snugly into the depression.

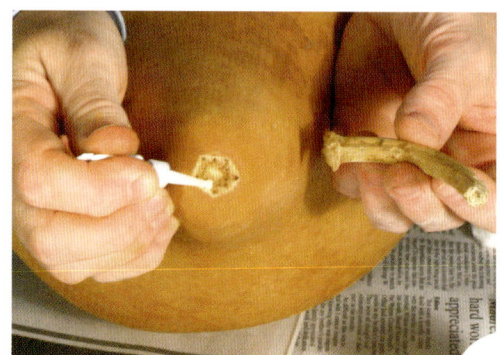

Super glue...

... is used to replace a stem.

Q: I carved a little too deeply — or maybe hit a thin part of the shell — and there is a little hole in one of my chips. How do I repair it?

A: For small holes, just dab a bit of natural color wood putty into the chip. Stipple it a bit with a pencil point if it looks too "smooth." It should stain OK with the leather dye, and if not it will probably look even better after you apply shoe polish. As a last resort, there is always acrylic paint to adjust the color. And this really only is a solution for very tiny holes. See how complicated this is getting? Better to develop a light carving touch!

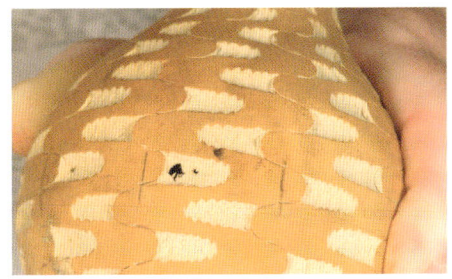

Small hole...

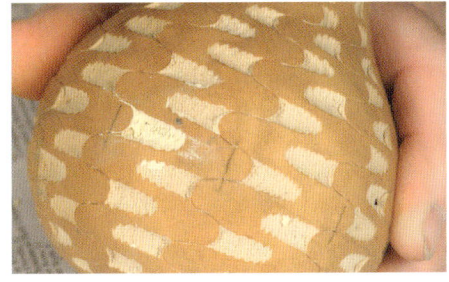

... fixed with wood putty.

Q: When I try to lay out circular patterns, the compass point makes tiny holds that show up as black dots when stained. If I change the location of the circle a few times until I get it right, I have a bunch of these dots. How can I prevent this?

A: Apply several layers of masking tape to the general area where you will be putting the compass point. The point will stay in the tape and not prick the surface. However be sure to remove any sticky residue from the gourd before staining, and do not try this on a gourd that has already been stained. *(Also if you are selling some of your beautiful stained gourd carvings, do not put self-adhesive price stickers on them since the adhesive will mar the finish. As a similar courtesy to your customers, send your gourds to their new homes in paper bags since plastic will also tend the pull a little of the finish, especially if the bag is placed in a hot vehicle.)*

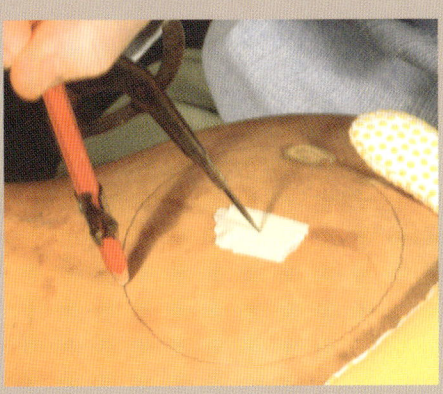

Masking tape is layered to prevent compass hole in gourd.

Q: Some of my older carved gourds have dust accumulated in the carving.

A: If buffing with a shoe brush does not help, just apply another coat of brown shoe polish. If there is light carving, avoid those areas by applying the polish with a toothbrush to just the dark carving.

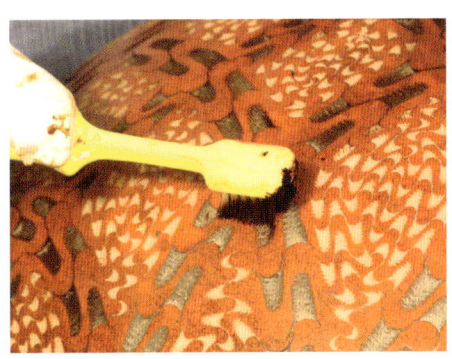

Polish over accumulated dust.

Q: You use a lot of brown — can't I add some color?

A: Sure! Leather dye comes in a wide range of colors. And, of course, you can use any product that is designed for wood since the dried gourd is essentially a wooden surface. You may want to test the product first, remembering that the object of staining is to make a better contrast between the carving and the background.

Another option is to add color to the light carving with watercolor. Since the interior is so fibrous, just paint across a small area of the light carving with watercolor and then dab quickly with a cotton ball to absorb the excess. The wax from the brown shoe polish will make the water bead up for easy removal. This does not work with acrylic paint.

Use watercolors to add color to light carving.

Q: Can I add more carving to a piece I thought was finished?

A: Yes. Remember the gourd with the three rows of diamonds? Suppose you decide there should be a fourth row of diamonds at the top — with light carving. Carve the diamond lines, and apply stain to the lines with a paintbrush. Dab quickly with a cotton ball. Dab to remove any excess — don't rub. If you just apply a small amount of stain at a time, there shouldn't be a problem since the line acts like a gutter. Once the excess stain has been removed, add the light carving to the diamond.

Add more carving to this "finished" gourd?

Carve lines for a top row of diamonds.

Add stain with a small paintbrush and then blot with a cotton ball.

Light carving added.

Q: I like to make small ornaments to sit on a shelf or be displayed in a bowl, but people want to hang them. Suggestions?

A: If the gourd has a stem, just tie a ribbon bow, with an extra loop for hanging tightly around the stem. If the stem is missing, insert a brass screw eye or cup hook bent to make an "eye." *(Best suggestion is to tell this "how to hang" information to buyers, otherwise you will spend a lot of time untangling ribbons when you set up for shows.)*

Ribbon hanging loops.

Add screw eyes or bent cup hooks.

Q: I want to make birdhouses to sell at craft shows. What is a good way to display them?

A: Your birdhouses will look best hung. A hall tree is an easy way to display 12-15 birdhouses at a comfortable height for shoppers.

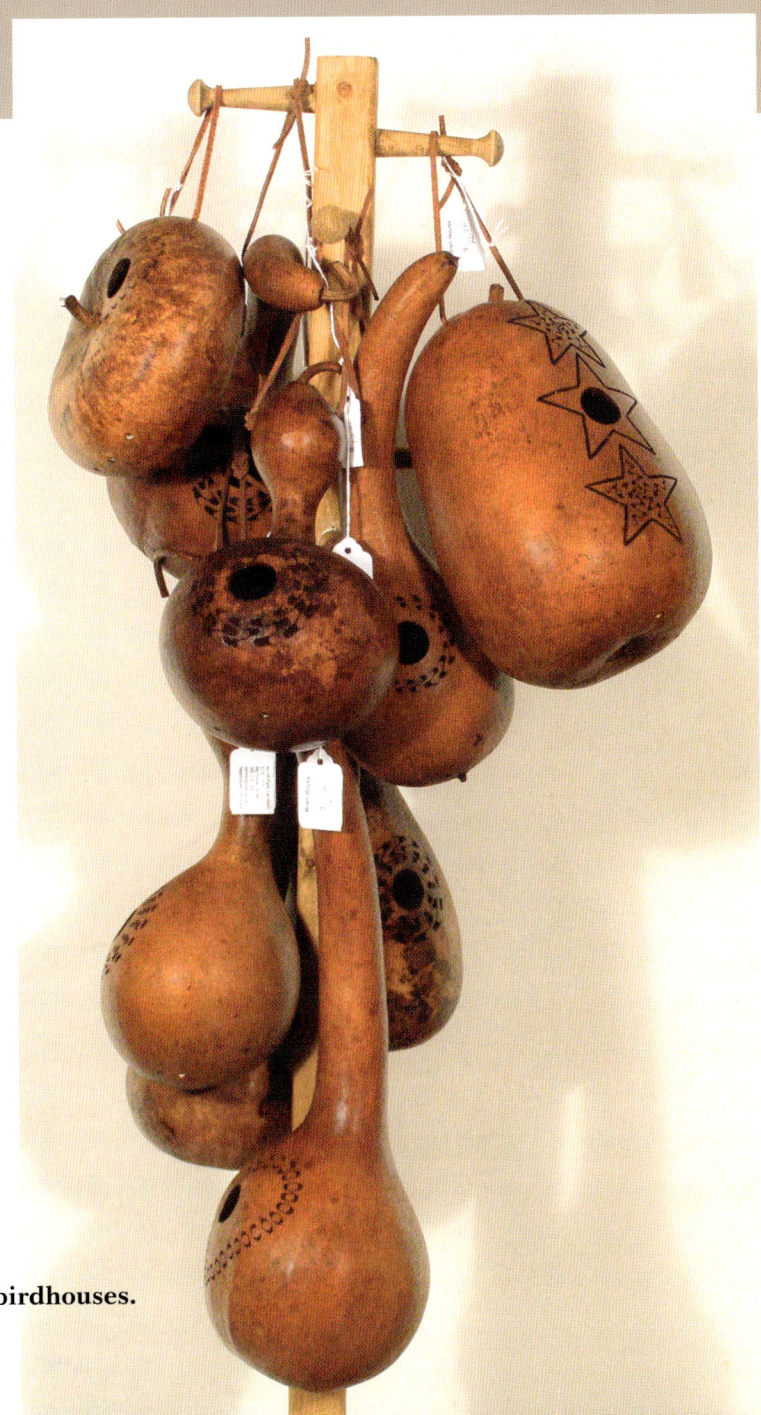

Hall tree...

... for displaying birdhouses.

CHAPTER EIGHT
GALLERY

I am pleased to showcase gourds carved by my father, who was my teacher, as well as by former students who have kept in touch over the years and have graciously shared photos of their work. Be inspired by the ways they have embellished basic carved lines and chips with their artistic insight!

An electric gourd lamp that was carved by Leslie Miller. The regular size light bulb is mounted on the circular wood platform. The lamp is 15 inches high and has small pinpricks in the white star outlines.

Necklaces by Katie McCormick.

Bowl with light carving and jewel inset. Artistry of Jill Nelson

This birdhouse has a simply elegant twining design. Lynn Quinn carved it with a 1/8-inch gouge.

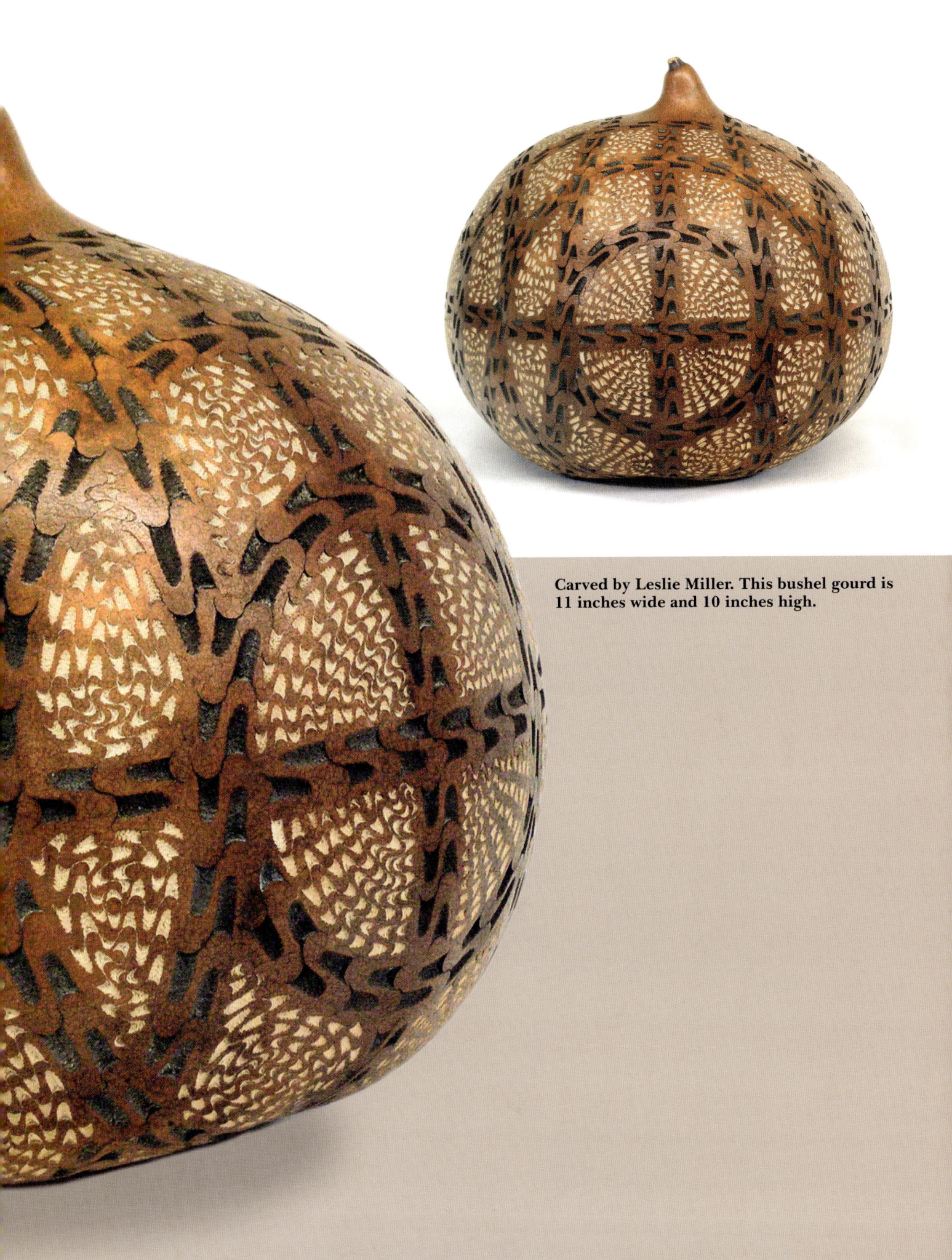

Carved by Leslie Miller. This bushel gourd is 11 inches wide and 10 inches high.

Carved and photographed by Gloria Riegel.

Ornaments 2 to 2 1/2 inches high.
Carved by Jeremy Rehm.

"Gate" birdhouses. Carved by Katie McCormick; she used a 3/16-inch gouge on 7-inch kettle gourds.

"Endless Circles" carved by Leslie Miller. This is a bushel gourd 15 inches wide and 13 inches high.

Carved and photographed by Gloria Riegel.

Celtic design. *Carved and photographed by A. B. Amis.*

Carved and photographed by Gloria Riegel.

Carved and photographed by Gloria Riegel.

Gourd Fun for Everyone. Sammie Crawford. Discover a world of enchantment and creative possibilities with Sammie Crawford, the Fairy Gourdmother. Her painting and decorating techniques, patterns, and practical instruction will have you creating masterpieces. Eight step-by-step projects are shown to get you started, and there are lots of other examples to inspire your own ideas of what a gourd can be.

Size: 8 1/2" X 11" 239 color photos 128 pp.
ISBN: 978-0-7643-3124-4 soft cover $22.99

Gourd Crafts: 6 Projects & Patterns. Ro Shillingford. Over 220 color photos and text guide readers through every step needed to create gourd bird houses, bowls, apple boxes, whimsy-bird vases, ewers, and scarecrow roly-polys. The text provides information on growing, curing, and cleaning gourds. Cutting and cleaning techniques, how to transfer pattern drawings, and gourd decoration are covered. Pattern drawings and a resources guide are supplied.

Size: 8 1/2" x 11" 222 color photos 64 pp.
ISBN: 978-0-7643-2825-1 soft cover $14.95

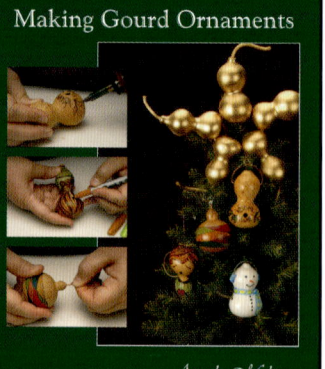

Making Gourd Ornaments. Angela Mohr. Clear instructions and 162 color photos teach readers to create Christmas ornaments from miniature, hard-shelled gourds. Designs include birdhouses, snowmen, angels, tree balls, tree toppers, and wall hangings. Instructions proceed from initial gourd cleaning to final painting, wood burning, and the installation of hangers.

Size: 8 1/2" x 11" 162 color photos 64 pp.
ISBN: 978-0-7643-2716-2 soft cover $12.95

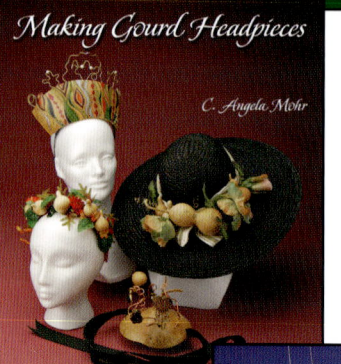

Making Gourd Headpieces: Decorating and Creating Headgear for Every Occasion. Angela Mohr. With simple tools and supplies already in the house or from the local craft shop, the author demonstrates how to make a variety of tiaras, barrettes, seasonal headbands, and hatpins from pieces of gourds. In fact, with a gourd thinking cap, like the one shown in this book, you can create your own from gourd parts.

Size: 8 1/2' x 11" 259 color photos 64 pp.
ISBN: 978-0-7643-2869-5 soft cover $14.95

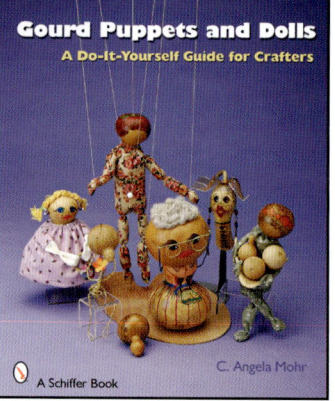

Gourd Puppets and Dolls: A Do-It-Yourself for Crafters. Angela Mohr. These projects join two age-old skills: gourding and sewing. With simple techniques, you can combine gourds with a cloth body to make dolls or puppets to enjoy or give as gifts. Learn how to make a gourd ragdoll, reversible dolls, marionettes, even bobble gourdheads!

Size: 8 1/2" x 11" 233 color photos 64 pp.
ISBN: 978-0-7643-2868-8 soft cover $14.95